Comfort and Joy

A comedy

Mike Harding

Samuel French — London
New York - Toronto - Hollywood

COMFORT AND JOY

First presented at the Oldham Coliseum on 16th May 1997, with the following cast:

Goff	Keith Clifford
Margaret	Meg Johnson
Helen	Jo-Anne Knowles
Martin	Colum Gallivan
Fiona	Deirdre Costello
Jimmy	Eric Potts
Chapman	Jeffrey Longmore
Monica	Irene Skillington
Kathy	Kathryn Dow Blyton
Crispin	Michael Remick
Pat	Irene Skillington
Hughie	Jeffrey Longmore

Director Kenneth Alan Taylor
Designer Celia Perkins
Lighting Designer Mark Howarth

COPYRIGHT INFORMATION

(See also page ii)

CHARACTERS

Goff
Margaret
Helen
Martin
Fiona
Jimmy
Chapman
Monica
Kathy
Crispin
Pat
Hughie

The action of the play takes place in the front room of the home of Martin and Margaret Duggan, in the north of England

Time — the present

SYNOPSIS OF SCENES

CHARACTERS

Goff He is in his seventies though very fit and spry. He is a retired railwayman who worked on the railways from demob in 1949 until retirement. He is a bit of a rogue but quite likeable though he does have a terribly annoying habit of repeating himself. He is a Lord of Misrule and takes no prisoners though he does have a soft underbelly.

Martin He is in his early fifties. He is Dublin Irish but has been in Britain for more than thirty years. He has done well on the building sites and now is site manager for a big construction firm. He is quick and witty, a real Dub/Jackeen. He is often light where Goff is dark. He is very likeable — but prone to talk politics when under the influence.

Margaret Martin's wife, Goff's niece. She is also in her early fifties and is very much the matriarch. She works as a secretary in a wholesale stationers; to her it is just a job and the focus of her life is her family. Like many women she is the family lynchpin, remembering birthdays, presents, et cetera.

Helen Martin's and Margaret's daughter. She is in her late twenties and teaches English at a school in Yorkshire. Pretty and intelligent, she has a wickedly dry sense of humour and is obviously more than a match for any man which is probably why Sean jilted her and ran off to have his nipples pierced and live with a halitosistic Mounted Police lady. Helen is very into aromatherapy and is quite hippy-like and Earth Mother-ish in the way she dresses, with long hair in a pony-tail, earth shoes, et cetera.

Kathleen (Kathy) Helen's sister, two years older. She is a style queen living in London, working as a funding officer for various art projects. She is very Post-Modern and feminist and is often more than anybody can handle. She has largely lost her accent and is brittle and pretentious, jerky and speedy; a northern Janet Street-Porter. Her clothes are very much whatever is "in".

Crispin He is an arts administrator and curator, ex-public school. He is from the Home Counties and, even though he tries very hard to be eclectic, his background comes through all the time. He is basically a pudding and since he is based on several people I know the actor playing him can show no mercy. Physically he should be the total opposite of Martin so that when he has to wear Martin's clothes he looks ridiculous. This is of course symbolic.

Jimmy The man who ran off to Australia with Goff's daughter Fiona. He is in his fifties and is bald but for a fringe which he combs over à la Charlton. He is quite portly now. He is cheerful and open in many ways but very much a product of the "I went to Australia and made my way" school. His accent is unbelievable (this is very important and cannot be conveyed in print): an exact fifty-fifty mixture of broad Oldham and Australian and a challenge for any actor.

Fiona The daughter who ran off with Jimmy; the woman who married the man from the "I went to Australia and made my way" school. She has not weathered well, is overweight and quite slow on the uptake. Her accent is very Australian, with just the occasional glimpse of the North.

Monica and **Chapman** They are ultra-ultra-respectable, the archetypal retired middle-class couple from Middle England. They dress modestly, but very expensively, and their appearance is very clean, neat and shiny; both are well-coiffured. They are also, of course, as we discover, stone barking mad.

Pat and **Hughie** Pat is similar to Margaret in dress and appearance though better preserved than Fiona. Hughie is gormless and vacant, so that one suspects that there is nothing going on inside his head; Pat, though, is very, very sharp. Their brief foray into ACT II SCENE 3 should end up quite fiery.

Mike Harding

Other plays by Mike Harding published by Samuel French Ltd:

Fur Coat and No Knickers
Last Tango in Whitby
Not With a Bang

ACT I

December 23rd. Evening

The front room of Martin and Margaret Duggan's comfortable and fairly large modern house in the north of England. Doors lead to the kitchen (part of which is visible through a hatch) and to the hall. There is a settee, an armchair, a television with remote control unit, a drinks cabinet, a telephone and an aquarium with stick insects in it (under the hatch) among the other furnishings

When the CURTAIN *rises, the television is on silently; the light from the screen flickers on the set. Goff is sitting in the armchair dressed in full Santa Claus outfit, with his feet up and a can of Boddington's and a glass in his hands. He starts to pour himself a pint*

The doorbell rings. A dog starts yapping loudly, off

Goff groans, puts the glass down, goes to the kitchen door and kicks it

Goff Will you shut up, you nowty little bugger!

The dog shuts up

Goff exits into the hall

Children's voices come from outside the door. We never see any of the various groups of children in this scene and in fact all their voices and cues could be taped or on mini-disc. The singing tails off miserably towards the end

Children (*off; singing*) We wish you a Merry Christmas
We wish you a Merry Christmas
We wish you a Merry Christmas
And a Happy New Year.
(*Speaking*) Compliments of the season.
Goff (*off*) Is that it?
Child (*off*) What?
Goff (*off*) Is that all you're going to sing? I want more for me fifty p than that. Come on, give us another one. Give us another one.

Children (*off; singing*) We three kings of Orient are
                                    Bearing gifts we travel afar
                                    Moor and mountain ... (*The singing tails off again*)
Goff (*off*) Go on .....
Children (*off; gathering courage as they sing, though the words are wrong*)
                                    Rudolph the Red-Nosed Reindeer
                                    Had a very shiny nose
                                    And if you ever saw him you would even say it glowed
                                    All of the other reindeers
                                    Wouldn't let him join in their games...

*The singing falters to a stop again. There is a long silence, then very strongly
they all sing out at the tops of their voices*

                                    So here it is Merry Christmas, everybody's having fun!!

We hear the door slam, off

Goff Bloody rubbish! Bloody rubbish!

Goff enters the front room

Three lines of half a poxy song and they've got their hands out for money.
They don't know one single carol all the way through. And if you give 'em
fifty p they stare at you as though you've crapped in their hats. It's the same
at Halloween; "Trick or Treat!" they shout now. Trick or bloody treat! And
on Bonfire Night if you don't give them a couple of quid for their Guy
Fawkes, your bloody garden gate ends up on the bonfire. Little buggers.
Merry Christmas. I'll give them Merry bloody Christmas. (*He goes back
to his seat and pours out the rest of the beer. He lifts up his beard, takes a
few contented sips of the beer and flicks channels with the television's
remote control unit. He is just about to relax when ...*)

*The doorbell rings again. The dog again does its "Hound from the Planet
Demented" act*

Shite and onions! You can't get five bloody minutes peace to yourself in
this house. (*He kicks the kitchen door again*) Shut up will you, you little
swine!

Goff exits to the front door

Children (*off; singing*)   Jingle bells, Jingle bells, Jingle all the way
                                    Oh, what fun it is to ride on a one-horse open sleigh
                                    Jingle bells, Jingle bells, Jingle all the way
                                    Hurrah for dear old Santa Claus
                                    Hurrah for Christmas Day
(*Straight into:*)
                                    We wish you a Happy Christmas
                                    We wish you a Happy Christmas
                                    We wish you a Happy Christmas
                                    And a Happy New Year.

There is a long, long silence

Goff (*off*) Same to you. Here you are, ten p each and that's all you're getting. You were crap, better than the last lot but still crap; if it wasn't Christmas you'd 'ave got bugger all — bugger all.

There is a long silence

Children (*off*) Miserable old bugger! Up yours grand-dad!

The door slams, off

Goff enters

Goff Cheeky little sods. (*He goes back to his chair, settles himself comfortably and flicks through the television channels with the remote control*)

The doorbell rings again

(*Leaping up, running and kicking the kitchen door, even though there is no barking*) SHUT UP YOU LITTLE SWINE!

He exits into the hall; we hear the front door open

The following line tails off towards the end

(*Off*) SOD OFF AND GET KNOTTED!   AND YOU CAN SHOVE CHRISTMAS where the monkey shoves his nuts ... (*He coughs, embarrassed*)

There is a long silence, then the choir of St John Boscoe strikes up with "Silent Night", very beautifully, but breaks down into fits of giggles and laughter

(*Off*) Evening, Father Conroy. Thought it was some kids; they've been very troublesome this evening. Very troublesome.

We hear money going into a collecting box

Goff comes back into the room

The dog barks dementedly

(*Moving to the kitchen door or hatch; very quietly and slowly*) Will you be quiet, please?

The dog shuts up. Goff, stunned, crosses the room and flops into his chair. For a while he is speechless; then, as he realizes the enormity of what he has just done he moans in a quiet, subdued voice

Oh shite. Oh shite. Oh shite and onions. (*A long beat*) Oh shite. Dear me. Hell fire. Oh shite. Onions. Shite and onions.

The above becomes a mantra and should and can go on for as long as the laughs are coming, with Goff staring glumly at the TV, cursing and flicking through the channels

Margaret enters with four full Tesco bags

Margaret Are you going to sit there staring at the telly all afternoon while we carry all this stuff in?
Goff No, no. (*He jumps up*) I'll give you a hand, love, no problem, right away. Where is it all? Let me at it.
Margaret Are you all right?
Goff Course I am, why?
Margaret Well, I normally have to ask you three or four times, that's why, and even then you only carry two bags before your back gives in.
Goff Well, it's Christmas, isn't it? Season of goodwill to all men and helping ladies in with the hard-won groceries. (*With an element of sarcasm*) I don't know how you women do it, I really don't, all that washing and babies and shopping and stuff: I think you should all be given medals.
Margaret Don't be so sarky. If we relied on you lot to do anything we'd be in a fine pickle; that one of mine could burn water. Men! Their bloody mothers ruin them and we have to pick up the pieces. (*She puts down her bags*) What are you doing still dressed like that?
Goff (*opening his red coat to show his vest and long johns*) Some bugger pinched me jacket and trousers.

Margaret At the old folks' home!

Goff I got changed in the kitchen and they reckon somebody came in while I were giving out the presents and nicked 'em. You can't leave anything down there. Anyway that's the last time I'll be doing it. I nearly ruptured meself carrying that sack from the kitchen to the day room. They should buy them lighter presents — half a ton of Black Magic and hairdryers. (*Beat*) And they were all asleep dribbling on their zimmer frames when I got there anyroad.

Margaret Did it go all right though?

Goff Did it buggery — there were a false fire alarm half-way through *Little Donkey*. Everybody panicked and there was a wheelchair and zimmer frame gridlock near the hot plate cupboard. God knows what'll happen if they ever have the real thing. I've told the warden it's the last time I'm doing it. I don't like being round old people, they depress me. I want to be beaten to death by a jealous husband when I'm ninety. (*Beat*) Trouble is there's only fifteen years to go.

Margaret We've just seen Father Conroy and the St John Boscoe's choir up the road. Three of the women were crying and two of the blokes were holding each other up under the lamp-post laughing. They looked as though they'd been drinking to me.

Goff (*ignoring her*) Where's Helen?

Margaret She's getting the stuff out of the car. Now come on if you're going to help. I've got that much to do I don't know whether I'm coming or going.

For the next few minutes, Goff, Margaret and Helen variously rush in and out of the house returning with Tesco bags until the room is nearly full. Finally they survey the mountain

I'll put the car away. Get the kettle on I'm gasping.

Helen It's disgusting. It makes me sick looking at it.

Goff The car? I thought it were new! It's one of them Toyotas, isn't it? They're supposed to be good.

Helen No, not the car, all this stuff. All this food and booze. More than two hundred pound this lot came to and it'll all be gone by Boxing Day. Half the world's starving and our bins are full.

Margaret (*heading for the exit*) Don't be such a weary willy, it's Christmas for God's sake. Go on, put the kettle on while I shift the car.

Margaret exits

Goff I'll put it on.

Helen I wouldn't mind if people took it seriously but the choir's just staggered down the street falling about laughing and looking like they're half-sozzled and they're the kind of people who are supposed to take Christmas seriously. Father Conroy doesn't think it's funny. He's got a face like a well-smacked bum. What are you doing still dressed like that anyway, Goff?

Goff I've decided that this is me role from now on: bringer of joy and happiness to the world, bringer of hope, a light in the darkness of our dismal daily lives. (*Beat*) Some thieving geriatric swine stole me clothes. The home's going to claim on their insurance; they told me to go out and buy a new suit and bring a receipt.

Margaret enters

Margaret Did Fiona phone?

Goff Nobody phoned.

Margaret Well I expect they'll phone from the airport when they get into London. She did say she was going to phone before they got the shuttle.

Goff is strangely silent and morose throughout this

It's a shame the kids couldn't have come as well, but it's like she said: it's not just the expense of getting them over here, it's what you do with them when they're here. Anyway they're old enough to be left on their own now.

Goff They could've all stayed where they are for me.

Margaret Goff, that's awful! That's your own daughter you're talking about there.

Goff Well what's that got to do with it?

Margaret She's your own flesh and blood.

Goff So was Lizzie Borden.

Margaret Come again? We've had no Lizzies in our family as far as I know. We had two Lilys but no Lizzie.

Helen Goff, who the hell are you talking about?

Margaret Are you thinking of her who ran that massage parlour on Union Street? Her that got caught by the VAT man when she tried to claim for a trouser press and four gallons of baby oil?

Goff Is it buggery! Is it buggery!

During the following, Goff goes into the kitchen and moves to and fro, passing the tea things through the hatch, sticking his head put of the hatch to talk

Lizzie Borden was American, a famous murderess. Oh, she were flesh and blood to her mam and dad all right. Happy families they were, I don't think.

It's "Yes Mam, yes Dad, no Mam, no Dad," all the time. Good as gold was Lizzie. Off to church every Sunday pumping the harmonium. (*He comes back in the front room now working himself up, gesturing and miming, talking a lot with his hands as always*) No, listen to this — this is serious this is — she's at church every bloody Sunday wearing holes in the knees of her tights.

Helen They didn't have tights in them days.

Goff That's nowt to do with it; stockin's, tights, whatever, you know what I mean: don't be so contrary. Then one morning her mam 'n' dad're sat there having their breakfast, heads bending down taking the tops off their boiled eggs, just going to dip their soldiers, and in she comes with the axe and takes *their* tops off. "Wham bam thank you, Mam" (*beat*) "— and Dad."

Margaret You've got a slate loose you have. It was thirty years ago. You haven't seen her for thirty years and now she's coming home. She's your only daughter, for God's sake! Can't you forgive and forget?

Goff (*dourly, with a very low-pitched voice*) It killed her mother.

Helen Uncle Goff, it was a fifty-nine bus killed me Aunty Nora.

Goff If she hadn't been so depressed about our Fiona she would have been aware of it coming.

Margaret Goff, she ran in the road to save what she thought was a child only it was a bollard. It was because she had her reading glasses on. That's what killed her, wearing the wrong glasses. Your Fiona didn't do anything wrong, she just emigrated to Australia.

Goff She ran off with Jimmy Corcoran, a married man.

Helen Everybody does that nowadays, it's a national sport. It's no big deal any more. (*Beat*)

Goff He took my saw with him.

Margaret You don't know that.

Goff I'd just had it sharpened.

Margaret You might have misplaced it.

Goff It was in the shed on the Friday. He borrowed it to shorten his Aunty May's clothes prop on the Saturday and it never came back. Never come back. I saw him Sunday at eleven o'clock Mass "Have you finished with that saw?" I asked him. "Oh, yes," he said. "I'll get it back to you." He borrowed it Saturday, I saw him on Sunday; by Monday he was at Southampton docks with our Fiona and my saw. His wife come round and all she said was, "Good riddance to bad rubbish." I said, "Never mind all that — what about my saw?" (*Beat*) And she just laughed. She just laughed! She stood there on the doorstep and she just laughed. She were still laughing when she walked off down our street.

Margaret (*to herself*) Oh my God — I should have known it was going to be like this.

Goff A lifeguard at the baths. She could have done better for herself, could have done better. Lifeguard.

Margaret He wasn't a bad bloke.

Goff (*exploding*) He were bloody rubbish. Bloody rubbish. He used to ponce around at the shallow end, blowin' his whistle and giving out the rubber bricks, trying to look like Billy Fury — Billy bloody Fury, with his big stupid blonde quiff and his tight white trousers and T-shirt on. And there'd be that much chlorine in the water me eyes used to end up like a dog's bollocks after it's jumped a barbed wire fence.

Helen Trumpton! Trumpton!

We realize later what Helen means but for the moment this exclamation hangs in the air like a piece of Dadaist absurdity. Goff and Margaret stare at Helen for a moment, then Goff continues with his diatribe

Goff He didn't half think a lot of himself, that Jimmy Corcoran. But I knew where they come from, I knew. You can't fool me, I've been around too long for that. His grandmother used to sell black peas and dog fat door to door. And spend the money in Yate's Wine Lodge. "Wine Lodge Winnie", they used to call her. That's what kind of family he come from. Bloody rubbish, the lot on 'em. A trouser press.

Helen It's thirty years, Goff: isn't it time you made up?

Goff (*after a beat; low and measured*) Well, I'll not deny them. (*Beat*) And I'm not going to spoil anybody's Christmas, and family is family when all's said and done, but it's not going to be easy — it'll not be easy.

Margaret Nothing ever is easy, Goff; you'll just have to try and make an effort.

There is the sound of a car drawing up outside

Helen Here's me dad. Site foreman — a sight for sore eyes more like. I wonder what's coming through the door this time; cuddly toy, reading lamp, bag of cement, window frame, conveyor belt?

Martin backs in through the door hauling an enormous Christmas tree which jams immediately in the doorway. It should be just big enough to give him a lot of trouble and to give the audience the impression that it will never come in, though of course it does finally. For a while Goff, Helen and Margaret watch Martin in amazed silence as he hauls at the massive tree

Martin Don't just sit there watchin', will you? Come here, Goff, would you for the love of God, and give us a hand with this.

Goff It's a bit big, in't it?

Martin I got it off a couple of the lads on the site. They picked it up down in Derbyshire.

Goff Fell off a lorry, did it?

Martin Not at all. It fell off a mountain. A couple of the lads took one of the site lorries and a chain saw out for a walk yesterday morning and came back with fifty of these. Our Christmas tree is courtesy of Lord Derbyshire. So thank you very much m'lud and a Merry Christmas to you and Mrs Derbyshire and all the little Derbyshires.

Helen That's robbery, Dad; just the same as stealing.

Martin He won't miss a bloody Christmas tree with all the millions he's got. Anyway where did he get the land from in the first place? Only by robbin' it off the people. He didn't go into a mountain shop and say (*cod English accent*) "Two mountains and a river please, my good man. And while I'm at it I'll have that forest on the top shelf. Don't bother wrappin' them, I'll take them now." He put bloody fences round the mountains and called them his. And with the help of his cronies in Parliament. Thievin' swine.

Goff It wouldn't be Christmas without a historical reappraisal of the role capitalism has played in world history.

Martin Anyway think of it as the redistribution of wealth. I'm only doing me own little bit to reverse the pernicious influence of Thatcherism and the "me" society. (*Beat*) Every Christmas tree we've ever had in the house has found its way here by the process of Marxist dialectics. Anyway, Goff, Peggy; would you ever come over here and give us a pull on this?

They all pull on the tree. The phone rings. Margaret goes to answer it. The others stand waiting and listening. We are to think from Goff's reaction that the call is from Australia or the airport. It is not

Margaret Yes. ... No. ... Oh, yes. ... It doesn't sound like you, it must be the line. (*She puts her hand over the mouthpiece and speaks to the others*) It's our Kath. (*Into the phone*) No, that's fine. ... Yes, your dad's here, and Helen. She got here this morning — and Uncle Goff. We're just going to put the decorations up. ... Well, no (*with doubt in her voice*) no, that's no problem, we'll find somewhere for him, providing he doesn't want a bedroom to himself. We'll sort something out. He might have to sleep on the settee. (*There is a long long beat, then she takes a very deep breath*) Oh. ... Oh. ... You can't get them in. ... Well, I suppose 'cos it's Christmas they'll all be full.

Helen (*mouthing to Martin and Goff; sotto voce*) The cats.

Martin (*to the ceiling*) The friggin' cats. Holy mother of God, she's bringing the friggin' cats and (*he nods towards Helen*) she's brought the friggin' dog.

Helen The dog was here first!

Margaret (*to the room*) Will you lot shut up, I can't hear a blessed thing! (*Into the phone*) No, that's smashing love. ... Fine. ... No problem. ... Anything you like. ... We've got plenty. ... Just bring what you want. ... Lovely. ... Yes. Lovely. ... Yes. ... Yes. ... Yes. ... Yes. (*A long beat*) No. ... Yes. Well (*she looks at Martin*) I got him them but I don't know if they'll fit; if they don't he'll just have to take them back and gerrum changed. All right, love. ... Yes. ... Lovely. ... Bye.

Martin So I know what I'm getting for Christmas now; more friggin' underpants.

Margaret You need new underpants.

Martin Only because you keep using the ones I have as dusters.

Margaret They're full of holes.

Martin Not all of them — and not all over, anyway.

Margaret They're disgusting.

Martin They're clean.

Margaret What if you get knocked down?

Martin If I'm lying there under a lorry like twelve stones of strawberry jam I won't exactly be worryin' about the condition of me Y-fronts, will I?

Margaret silently stares at Martin for a brief moment, wondering whether the argument is worth pursuing

Helen (*who is used to all this*) What did she say?

Goff She's bringing the cats, then?

Margaret The usual cattery's closed down because of a bereavement. Apparently the woman who owns it had a massive heart attack in Santa's grotto and dropped dead in the bran tub. And every other cattery in London is full.

Martin What the hell was the woman who runs the cattery doing in Santa's grotto?

Margaret It seems that as well as running a cattery she was a dwarf. And she was working part-time as one of Santa's Little Helpers. There was a queue of kids a mile long. They've been terribly upset. They've had to have counselling. (*Beat*)

Goff (*seriously*) Dangerous job being Father Christmas nowadays. If they aren't pinching your gear you're having heart attacks and ending up in the bran tub.

Helen (*as before*) Trumpton! Trumpton!

The others look at Helen

Margaret And she's bringing a friend with her — to stay.

Martin A boyfriend?

Margaret No, Martin, not a boyfriend — he's just a friend. She says he's keen on her but she just wants him as a friend. He's got nowhere to go for Christmas and she feels sorry for him. She says he's very nice. He's from Basildon and he's called Crispin. Oh my God! I'll have to rush out and get him a present before the shops close.

Helen We'll all have to get him a present. God knows what he's like. If he's anything like our Kath's usual friends he'll be a right drip.

Goff Harsh — but fair.

Martin Crispin? What kind of a name is that?

Margaret It's a very nice name. St Crispin. He runs an art gallery.

Goff St Crispin runs an art gallery?

Helen He's probably a spoilt Southern ex-public schoolboy who's worked his way into the modern art world and who does installations that are very *au fait* and Post-Modern and understood by eleven people worldwide.

Goff He'll be full of bullshit like that what's-his-name, that Tarquin that she brought up last Easter. What was it he did? I couldn't make head nor tail of it. I couldn't decide in the end whether it was total rubbish or absolute rubbish.

Martin (*quoting in the style of The South Bank Show*) "He was a Post-Modernist playwright who wrote plays with no beginning and no end in which the actors could move in and out of the action choosing whatever character they wanted to play, sometimes changing character in the middle of a speech. Part signifier and part signified, the actor or actors would often change roles with the audience, inviting them to carry on the play while the actors went home."

Goff How could you remember all that?

Martin Love of God, how could anyone forget it?

Margaret Having played Long John Silver in the Margaret Mary's kids panto doesn't make you an expert on world theatre.

Martin I was doin' fine 'til I got me peg leg stuck down that knot hole on the stage and went arse over tip into Blind Pugh.

Goff I can still see you lying there shouting, "Don't just stand there, get me up, you dozy pillock", and Blind Pugh trying to pretend he couldn't see you and get you up at the same time. One of the great theatrical moments of all time in my book was watching them saw the end off your peg leg so the show could go on while Blind Pugh sang "Yo Ho Ho and a Bottle of Rum" followed by (*he stands and mimes*) "I Did It My Way". Anyway, come on, let's get this bloody tree in.

They all pull on the tree. We hear the sound of another group of children assembling outside; this time they sing the theme "Walking in the Air" from The Snowman. Everyone onstage stops pulling to listen. There is something very beautiful about the singing and there is a very special little moment as a clear child's voice rings out over the scene. Everyone onstage is quite visibly moved

Martin peers over the top of the tree, perhaps standing on a chair to see

Martin It's a friggin' tape recorder. (*To the offstage children*) Bugger off you cheatin' little swine! (*To the adults*) They're out there with a friggin' ghetto blaster; one holdin' the ghetto blaster, the other two with collectin' boxes. (*To the children*) Bugger off — you must think we're soft. (*Alone and with no effort at all he pulls the tree in and stands it up*)

The tree is massive

Margaret It's a bit big!
Martin Aw, come on, it was only a fiver.
Helen It's hitting the ceiling.
Margaret You'll have to cut a bit off.
Martin Me saw's at work

Beat

Goff Mine's in Australia.
Margaret (*very sharply*) Will you shut up about that blinking saw! (*Referring to the tree*) What are we going to put it in?
Martin We'll fill a bin with bricks and stand it in that — there'll be no problem. Job's a good 'un. (*He rubs his hands in a businesslike manner*) Dig deep and throw well back. Up the yard, Paddy, there's a hum of hay off you.
Helen Well, we'll put the stuff away while you sort it out.

"Deck the Halls" begins to play, followed by a medley of other Christmas hits. During this, the shopping is removed, the tree is erected and decorated and other decorations are put up around the room. This process is very swift and is choreographed to the music. When the music stops the set has been transformed into a decorated family home with all the trimmings

Margaret That's nice, really lovely.
Martin The angel got bent last year and it won't go back on the top.
Helen It was that fool McGoldrick that trod on it.
Martin It wasn't his fault the tree fell down.
Margaret No, it was his drunken wife, that what's-her-name, Funnelola or whatever it is.
Martin Fionula and you know full well what her name is — you're just pretendin'.

Margaret Fionula. What a stupid name!

Martin It's a very old Irish name. It's the female version of Finn as in Finn McCool a great Irish hero. We had Irish heroes and Irish colleges and Irish schools and laws while you lot were still running round covered in woad shaking your spears at the Romans. Anyway you just didn't like her because she fancies me.

Margaret (*rising to the bait, and actually quite jealous*) Fancies you! Don't be ridiculous.

Martin I'm not that ugly! I haven't just fell off the bells at Notre Dame you know.

Margaret Anyway, don't flatter yourself: she fancies anything in pants — or out of them. Particularly out of them.

Goff To change the subject ever so slightly: does anybody fancy a drink?

Helen Gin and tonic please. Where's the dog?

Goff pours drinks during the following

Margaret I thought he was in. I'll have the same please, Goff.

Martin I'll have a small Black Bush with another one to keep it company in case it'd be lonely. (*He switches the tree lights on. Nothing happens*) The friggin' lights have gone again. They were brand new last year. I buy a new set of lights every friggin' year and twelve months later they're dead. They only have to work once a year, that's all, and they can't even do that. They're worse than your bloody queen — at least she *works* every Christmas.

Margaret And you can't take them back because they only cost you a fiver on the site. That's what you get for five-pound Christmas lights; they work from Christmas Eve to Twelfth Night and then it's "Good-night, Vienna." Sometimes, Martin Duggan, I get fed up with you and your blessed deals. Half the stuff in this house doesn't work because it fell off a lorry or you got it off a bloke on the site. I've had a new bathroom for nearly a year and I had me first bath in it last week. If we didn't have a shower as well I'd have been stood in the back yard with a scrubbin' brush.

Martin The bloke who had the taps was away.

Helen In Strangeways.

Margaret Taps — you're tapped! And I must have been to have married you!

Helen (*opening the door*) Trumpton! Trumpton!

Goff (*pouring drinks*) It might be just the fuse — try the fuse.

Margaret One of them bulbs is a fuse.

Martin What kind of a name for a dog is that — Trumpton? How can you take a dog like that seriously?

*We hear the dog coming up to the house and then running around inside it.
We never see the dog or the cats; all the action is created in the imagination
by the actors and through sound effects*

Goff He's well named in one respect; I've never smelt farts like 'em. Never.
I'll tell you! My God for a little dog he can't half pump. He can that! I mean
he must be, what, fifteen inches long if he's that and about seven inches
high, and he dropped one this morning that had me hair falling out. How
can such a little dog drop such huge farts? (*He is genuinely amazed at this
and becomes almost lyrical*) I mean I look at him and he looks like a normal
little dog: normal dog, you'd think nothin' of it, just an everyday dog; tail,
fur, teeth, eyes, a bark, then — "foot!" (*He makes a dog farting noise*)

*Martin doesn't listen to any of the following since like all of them he can turn
Radio Goff off*

He drops one and you're smashing the windows to let some air in. And
there's hardly any noise: he just looks at you sly, lifts his tail a bit and the
next minute the wallpaper starts peeling off. It's him that's ruining the
ozone layer with his methane. He's deadly, that dog, deadly. He should be
put down for the sake of the planet.

Martin You can get away with a bit of silver paper or Bacofoil in the bulb
fuse holder. (*He finds a piece of Bacofoil and puts it into the bulb fuse
holder during the following*)

Helen (*looking through the hatch to the kitchen*) There's a good boy. Have
you had a good play out, then?

Goff What kind of a dog is he really? I mean, let's be serious, he's a right
Bitzer.

Helen Bitzer?

Goff Bitzer this, bitzer that.

Helen He's actually a Patterdale Border Manchester cross.

Goff He's a little fartbox; what do you feed him on, corpses?

Martin (*switching on the lights*) There you go!

*The Lights burn brightly and there are various admiring noises from the cast
as the Spirit of Christmas washes around the house. Goff brings over the
drinks he has just poured out*

Margaret Lovely; I'm dying for this.

Goff Here you are, the first Christmas drink. Merry Christmas, everybody.

All Merry Christmas.

*The room and tree lights flicker slowly at first, then flicker faster and faster.
There is a dull bang and the house is plunged into darkness. There is a long
beat*

Martin Feck!!

Helen You and your five-pound bloody lights.

Goff You should never let a joiner anywhere near electricity. Nowhere near the electric. Joiners are all right with wood and screws but keep 'em away from electrics.

Martin Would you ever shut up you auld bollix and strike a match or something.

Helen lights a lighter and they all wander round in the gloom bumping into each other

Margaret I knew it — I just knew it! I knew something was going to happen all bloody day.

Outside we hear a group of children gathering and singing "Away in a Manger"

All Will you bugger off!!!

There is silence

Black-out

SCENE 2

Christmas Eve. Morning

The Lights come up. Martin is lying on the settee, his body covered by his overcoat; under the coat, his flies are undone and he has a woman's bra on over his shirt. He has what is left of a party hat on his head and has lipstick on his face, which he doesn't notice. He is nursing a hangover the size of Hanover. During the following, the overcoat slips down to reveal the bra

Goff enters in a manner hateful to all hangover sufferers: bright and cheery. He is carrying a bag of greens. All through this scene Goff is loud and raucous, Martin quiet and suffering

Goff Ey up! The invasion of the creature from the Dyers and Polishers Club. "Will it live?" we ask ourselves, this thing from beyond, this alien fallen from on high to planet Earth. All that is left of a sinister genetic experiment to mate an extra-terrestrial with the sludge at the bottom of a Guinness barrel. The wages of sin.

Martin (*from his lying position; indistinctly*)Would you ever shut up, you auld bollix! Oh God, oh God, Holy Smoking Jaysus and Barney McGrew.

Oh the head! Oh God! (*He sits up*) Oh God! (*He lies down*) Oh, oh, oh, oh
God, oh feck! (*He sits up*) Oh, oh, oh, thunderin' Jaysus, oh God. (*He lies
down*).

Goff Are these those stomach flattening exercises you were telling me
about? They aren't working. You know what would set you up? A half-
done fried egg snotty side up, some cold baked beans and a bootlace of
burnt bacon.

Martin Oh God, oh shite. Shut up you, would you, for the love of God; give
us a break, you auld hoor. Oh, oh, oh, oh. (*He sits up; this time we think he's
going to be up for good but he opens his eyes, looks wildly around him and
lies slowly and gently down again*) Oh, Christ almighty! The head is
destroyed.

Goff Cup of tea? (*He goes to the kitchen*)

Martin I don't know if I'm man enough.

Goff I know the feeling, there's nothing worse, you don't know whether you
want to live or die. It's a terrible feeling, terrible feeling; I deeply
sympathize, said the Walrus.

Martin Yer a hard man Goff; anybody who'd kick you in the heart would
break their foot.

Goff (*sticking his head through the hatch*) They have a cure against
hangovers in North Africa. They eat giant slugs in ginger sauce. I saw it
when I were out there in the army. They take the slugs and dip 'em into
ginger sauce while they're still alive. Then they eat them, still alive; big
slugs ten inches long. (*He disappears, then reappears in the hatchway
scrunching a piece of celery; expansively*) In Hong Kong they eat the
brains of a live monkey while it is still living. They trepan it, you know cut
the top of its head off, and it's still alive; then they shake hands with it and
scoop its brains out.

Martin (*groaning*) Goff, for Jesus' sake will ya ——

Goff They even have a special table with a hole in it that the monkey's head
comes through. They have sauces with it of course, brains doesn't taste of
much; hoy sin, ginger and garlic, sweet and sour ——

Martin (*shouting*) Will you ... ?Aagh, Holy Whistling Moses and his
melodeon — the head. (*He lies down again*)

*Margaret enters wearing a pinny. During the following she tidies, dusts
and arranges things behind the settee — she doesn't see the bra on Martin
at this stage*

Margaret Oh, it found its way home did it? It's amazing, is this. The Dublin
homing pigeon: can find its way home, and has been doing so from various
booze-ups over the last thirty years, but somehow forgets what stairs are
for. Out of the taxi, through the door, coat off, then — shazzam — the

memory bank's erased and Starship Whatasurprise hits a forcefield of Klingons at the stair bottom and spends the night on the settee.

Martin I didn't want to wake you up.

Margaret Well, that's very kind and considerate of you, love, but you shouldn't have. You've no idea how much I look forward to watching you trying to get undressed when you're pretending not to be legless. There's nothing I love better than the "hop, skip and not a chance of a jump" dance you do when you're (*she relishes the phrase*) troubled with ale.

Martin My God, two comedians in the one house!

Margaret It's a sight that restores my faith in humanity, you pogoing round the bedroom trying to get a trouser leg over a foot. And of course the shirt buttons are completely beyond you once liquor mortis has set in. You forget the combination completely and they either end up ripped off, pinging all over the bedroom like a hailstorm or you spend half an hour choking to death trying to pull the shirt over your head.

Martin Give us a break woman, have yez no flamin' pity? Yer like a bloody Dalek on HRT!

Margaret But at least we were spared the "bacon butty and the smoke alarm going off" routine. That's always a good one. Particularly when you bring McGoldrick home and he tries to stop it by standing on my kitchen table and hitting it with an eggwhisk. I remember with great affection the morning I came down to find the crew of a fire tender sitting in my kitchen drinking cups of tea all watching McGoldrick trying to stick the smoke alarm back on the ceiling with a daub of Marmite. I didn't know I had so much laughter in me.

Martin There's too many gobshites in this house.

Margaret That's rich coming from you! I didn't know whether that was World War Three breaking out at half-past four this morning or just the man I married paying off a Pakistani taxi driver. If I heard *Here's me hand and here's me heart* once I heard it a million times; it went on for half an hour. That and United's chance in the cup. It's a wonder her next door didn't phone for the police like she did on Paddy's Night when you and them other idiots sang *Kevin Barry* and *Johnson's Motor Car* from the middle of her rhododendrons.

Martin (*quietly trying to justify himself*) We couldn't find our way out.

Margaret I wouldn't have minded if you finished the song — you didn't get through one verse without someone shouting "Revenge for Skibereen". So where were you last night then until four in the morning? Helping Santa oil the reindeer?

Martin I haven't a bloody clue.

Goff (*through the hatch*) Tea's up. (*He puts cups of tea on the hatchway*)

Margaret collects Martin's tea and comes round the front of the settee. She gives him his tea and notices the bra

Margaret An Ann Summers Party, was it? Funny, Martin, I'd never seen
   you as a white Wonderbra man meself, more a mucky black and red basque
   type with holes in the stockings ... more you I'd have thought.
Martin (*seeing the bra*) Wha ...? Jeezu ... ! Basta ... ! I'll murder them. It's
   them lot did it for a laugh.
Margaret I'm not laughing.

Goff comes into the front room

Goff (*seriously*) It's bloody daft is that; they could have got you into trouble.
Margaret (*icily*) They have.
Helen (*off*) Hallo ——

A dog barks, off

   We're back.
Goff Is it them?
Margaret They phoned from the airport an hour ago.
Goff Oh.

*During the following, Goff pours cups of tea, which we know is his way of
coping with the situation*

   Martin, without taking the bra off, goes out to help with the suitcases

Margaret stands by the door

   *Fiona enters followed by Jimmy, with Helen and Martin behind them.
   Jimmy is bald but for a fringe; Fiona is notable for having little sense of
   humour and for wearing flouncy, frilly clothes*

Margaret kisses Fiona and Jimmy

Margaret (*gibbering a bit because of her nerves*) Eeeh, it's good to see you.
   I bet you're tired after that long journey. Eeh, Fiona, love, you don't look
   any different. It must have been a long flight.

*The next part of the scene should contain holes and silences; more is left
unsaid than said. Though there is a lot of strain, we should feel that they are
muddling through*

Helen (*who is used to her mother going to pieces at emotional moments;
   matter-of-factly*) The airport was packed. There were thousands there, all

coming home for Christmas. Is there something you're trying to tell us, Dad?

Martin struggles out of the bra. Fiona and Jimmy stand open-mouthed for a moment, watching him struggle to get it off

Martin It was the lads' idea of a joke. We had the Christmas "do" last night.

There is a long silence. This should be sustained for as long as it will hold

Fiona Hallo, Dad.
Goff Hallo, love. You're looking well. (*A long beat*) I'd better make a fresh pot of tea for everybody.
Fiona (*going over to Goff*) You're looking well too, Dad; being retired must suit you.
Goff (*putting his arms around Fiona*) Oh, love. (*He breaks into tears*) It's good to see you, it really is.

There is a long beat

Margaret (*wiping her eyes*) I'll make some tea.

The dog starts yapping dementedly at something

Helen Trumpton, just shut up and behave, now there's a good boy. I'll do it, Mum. (*She goes into the kitchen*)

There is a long silence. Goff and Fiona are still in each other's arms

Martin You still support City then, Jimmy?
Jimmy Too bloody right, Martin — somebody in Australia has to.
Goff I were wrong though, I were wrong, but you know the way I am once I get something in me head, and I never liked writin' letters much anyhow. (*Beat*) But I read all yours.
Fiona It's all water under the bridge, Dad.
Martin (*wiping his eyes*) I don't fancy their chances for the cup, though.
Jimmy (*wiping his eyes*) Not unless they get rid of McDermot.
Martin (*still wiping his eyes*) He played like a big girl's blouse all last season.
Jimmy (*blowing his nose*) Half a million they paid for him.
Martin (*blowing his nose*) A waste of space. I wouldn't have paid half a million washers for him. (*Beat*) I'd better take your bags upstairs, get you settled in.
Margaret (*wiping hers again*) Not yet — let them get a cup of tea first.

Jimmy shakes Goff's hand

Jimmy All right, Goff.
Goff (*wiping his eyes*) Not bad, Jimmy, not bad.

There is a beat, during which Goff's eyes are fixed on Jimmy's head

    I see the quiff has gone Jimmy.
Jimmy The what?
Goff The Billy Fury hair do.
Jimmy Oh, right, the quiff! That went with the waistline an' th'eyesight an' everythin' else, Goff. Too much good livin'. A workin' man's paradise, Australia.
Martin You've done well for yourself, Jimmy — I saw the photos. Fair play to you. And you haven't lost your accent either.
Jimmy No. Fiona's lost hers, though. It's funny. Thirty years and they still ask me if I've just got off th' boat. The kids' friends think I'm Greek. No, it's a grand country, Martin. If you've got a half-decent job in Oz you can easily afford a decent house with a bit of land and your own swimming pool.
Goff (*after a beat*) Still do a bit o' life-guardin' then?
Jimmy (*laughing*) You don't forget anything, do you, Goff?
Goff (*glumly*) Not much.
Helen (*from the kitchen*) Here you are, a good strong pot of Yorkshire Gold.

Helen comes in with the tea and hands it round during the following

Jimmy only half-hears Goff's next line as he is reaching out for his tea

Goff You wouldn't remember anything about a saw, would you?
Jimmy Saw?
Margaret Give over, Goff, for heaven's sake; give us a break, do. Come on, Jimmy, sit down. Now would anybody like a biscuit or some cake?

They variously get themselves settled in chairs, on arms of chairs et cetera

Fiona We came in by town; I didn't recognize it. They've knocked it all down! There's only the Town Hall left that I recognize; the rest of it's all new. And that looks awful, too — it's all dirty grey stained concrete. And half the shops look closed. It's worse than it was when we left!
Martin It's what the experts call "Post-Modern."
Fiona It's what?
Margaret He watches a lot of Open University on BBC2 late at night.

Jimmy What's happened to all t' mills? My bloody oath! Half of them are gone and those that aren't gone don't look as though they're workin'.

Goff There's only Crompton and India working now; that's two left out of sixty-five.

Jimmy What about Jubilee?

Goff "Planet Beyond Space Disco."

Fiona Eagle?

Margaret Roller blade rink and go-kart track.

Jimmy Sudan?

Martin Architectural antique warehouse.

Fiona (*counting the names off on her fingers*) Then there was Liberty, Nelson, Broadgate, Cockrofts, Shiloh, Zion, Manchester, Turks ——

Goff (*counting them off on his fingers*) Knocked down, permanent craft fair and Tupperware Seconds Shop, Lazer Quest, knocked down, art gallery-cum-bistro-cum-performance space, knocked down, knocked down, knocking shop.

Helen It's not a knocking shop! It's "Albert Africa's 30-Plus Disco" now is Turks!

Goff That's what I said: it's a knocking shop.

Fiona It's really strange; it's like coming back to a foreign country. McDonalds, Pizza Hut, all the kids walking round in trainers and jeans and baseball hats on back to front; it's like being in America.

Goff Ay, that's what we are: the fifty-third bloody state, Englandland, USA. Coca-bloody-Cola and half the rubbish on television is American — or Australian. T' bloody "Hex Files" and "Oprah Winifred"! And that *Neighbours* — meks me want to put me bloody foot through the screen.

Martin You can see he's mellowed a lot over the years.

Goff (*ignoring Martin*) Ay, things've changed since you went off to Australia. They have that. What Hitler failed to do the bloody politicians finished off. I mean what did we fight a war for, that's what I want to know? For them to shut all t' mills and pits down and turn 'em into discos.

Margaret Part Two — "How I Bled For My Country".

Fiona I remember this one.

Martin He's got a point, though. Fair play to you, Goff — fire into it.

Goff Well, it's bloody right! It's right. Look at t' Japanese, look at t' bloody Japanese.

Margaret What about the Japanese?

Goff Cars, motorbikes, televisions, videos, cameras ... they're even making whisky now! Making bloody whisky! Glenwakisaki or what ever it's called. Richest country in t' world. And they're takin' over *your* shop!

Martin Ireland?

Goff (*indicating Jimmy*) No, his shop, Australia; they're in there like Flynn, like Flynn, buyin' up stuff.

Jimmy It's just inward investment, that's all it is.

Goff That's how it starts, that's how it starts — inward investment. First they build a car factory then they tell you if you don't join the EMU they'll piss off somewhere else with their money.

Fiona I thought emus were birds?

Margaret Come on, Fiona, I'll show you your room; this could go on for days. (*To Martin*) And you, don't you go getting involved in this; you can do something useful, you can give us a hand upstairs with these bags.

Fiona, Margaret and Martin exit

Helen I'll take Trumpton for a walk.

Helen exits

There is a long beat

Jimmy No, you've got it wrong, Goff, Australia is still for th' Australians. It's a reet grand country, my bloody oath it is.

Goff What Australians? The only real Australians I know about are the Aborigines and from what I've seen on the telly they haven't all got swimming pools and barbecues and good jobs.

Jimmy Well, it's the grog, partly. You see, your Abo can't take the grog. They've not got the right mentality. And if *they'd* have been left to run the place then nothing would have happened to it.

Goff So? It were their country, weren't it?

Jimmy What do you mean?

Goff The white man stole it off them, that's what I mean.

Jimmy It's destiny; you can't stop progress.

Goff Well, if *Neighbours*, *Home and Away*, *Skippy the* pigging *Kangaroo* and playing cricket lookin' like Darth piggin' Vader are progress I'll show me arse in the Vatican. Anyway I'm going on me allotment for some sprouts for tomorrow.

Jimmy (*perplexed at Goff's vehemence*) Right, fine.

Goff And while I'm gone see if you can remember anythin' about a saw.

Goff exits

Jimmy (*looking puzzled*) Saw? Saw?

Black-out

Christmas Eve. Evening

*The Lights come up. The Christmas tree is lit, the candles are lit and there
is a very Christmassy feeling*

*Martin, Helen, Margaret, Goff and Fiona enter with drinks. They seat
themselves, with Jimmy, more or less in the same positions as they occupied
when sitting in Scene 2. They are watching Morecambe and Wise on the TV.
We can't see the screen but can see the light from it flickering on their faces*

Martin You've never really settled have you, Jimmy?

Jimmy She 'as, like, but I've never settled really. I mean I like it like but I
miss it here. Like the football, I always try ter keep up wi' what City is doin'.
And me Aunty Mag used ter send the *Evening Post* every week 'til she died.

Goff Well, she couldn't send it after she were dead, could she?

Jimmy No, that's right enough, but yer know what I mean. It's the beer an'
all. Thirty years and I've never got used to the beer. Ice-cold gnat's pee,
stubbies and tinnies; you can't get a decent pint.

Fiona (*nodding towards the screen*) You know, I didn't know they were still
alive.

Goff The big one isn't.

Martin They were good though — they never did any filth, never went blue.

Goff They were funny, by they were funny. They did years on the boards;
that's where they learnt their comic timing. It's the most important thing
of all in comedy, is timing. (*Beat*) Tommy Cooper's dead.

Jimmy He were a wonderful boxer.

Martin Not the boxer, the comedian — (*he does a very poor impression, his
accent still broad Dub*) "Just like that — ha ha ha — just like that." You
remember him? He was gas.

Fiona No. (*A beat*) Is Arthur Askey dead? I never liked him. He had that
woman with huge breasts — that Sabrina — and he used to woggle his
spectacles. "Hallo Playmates", he used to go. I thought he was disgusting.

There is a long beat

Jimmy I used to like Mr Pastry. And *Dixon of Dock Green* : "Evenin' all!"
And that Harry Worth. (*He stands and puts out one arm and one leg like
Worth used to do at the beginning of the show*)

The others look at Jimmy

Fiona He was good, that Bruce Forsyth on *Sunday Night at the London Palladium*; is he still alive?
Goff Sort of.
Helen His wig is.
Fiona Is he still alive? What was it he used to say? (*She sticks her thumb up*) Swingin'.
Margaret That was Norman Vaughan.

Jimmy sings a couple of lines of "Give Me the Moonlight". The others look at Jimmy

Helen That was Frankie Vaughan, even I know that.
Martin He could sing a bit, that Frankie. (*He sings a few lines of the verse to "Give me the moonlight". Then, speaking*) They don't write 'em like that any more.
Fiona You've not lost your voice, Martin.
Martin Jimmy used to sing a bit, didn't you Jimmy? What was the name of that group you used to sing with down at the *Moulders*?
Jimmy "Einstein and the Atom Smashers".
Margaret We used to think they were wonderful. We followed them all over: Bury, Bolton, Royton, Eccles, Rochdale. We used to tell our mams and dads we were stopping at each others' houses and we'd go off on all-night raves. We thought it was very daring. I used to have me hair done up in a beehive and shoes with heels you could have drilled for oil with. Do you remember them, Fiona? And the paper-nylon underskirts that you used to stiffen with sugar in the bath.

There is a beat while they think on their memories

Goff There's a group called *The Saw Doctors* now.
Martin They're Irish, from County Galway somewhere.
Helen They're good; I saw them live at college.
Goff It's an interesting name, *The Saw Doctors*.
Margaret Goff — give us a break.

The doorbell rings

Who the heck's this at this time on Christmas Eve?
Martin It'll be the new people next door but one. I saw him out power-hosing his garden ornaments this mornin' and told them to come round for a drink tonight.
Helen It's not the house with the peeing manikin and the windmill and all the other tatty stuff, is it?

Martin The very one. Thirty-seven gnomes following various pursuits including fishing, playing banjos and pushing wheelbarrows. And a rake of plaster of Paris herons standing over a pond the size of a spilt pint.

Margaret Well, you can go and get the door.

The bell rings again

Martin goes

I'll swing for him one of these days. Last year he got that drunk that he invited anybody in who knocked on the damn door. They were all comin' round for their Christmas boxes, postmen, dustbin men, all of them. I came home with a car full of shopping and he's making bacon butties for three paperboys, two postmen, four dustmen, three window cleaners and a coal man, and half of them weren't ours — particularly the coal man. We've been all gas for years!

Martin, Chapman and Monica can be heard, off. They enter during the following lines

Martin ... for the time of year.

Chapman Thought it might have broken by now.

Monica Well, with the frost this morning I thought we might have got snow.

Martin (*to the family*) This is Monica and Chapman, everybody, from next door but three.

Monica *Cap de Lune.*

Goff What?

Monica It's the name of the house. We've had such lovely times there on holiday that we called it *Cap de Lune.*

Martin, Chapman and Monica sit down, Chapman and Monica to either side of Goff. Helen turns the TV off

Martin This is my wife Margaret; that's Fiona her cousin, Goff's daughter; this is Jimmy, her husband; that's Goff, he's Fiona's dad and Margaret's uncle, he lives in a bus shelter — I'm sorry — sheltered accommodation down the road.

Monica and Chapman do not react as they have no sense of humour

And this is Helen, our daughter; she's a teacher over in Knaresborough for her sins. Don't worry if you can't remember them all; I'll draw yez a map.

Monica Goodness, what a large family you seem to have!

Margaret There's more of them but they aren't all here. Another one's coming tomorrow.

Goff There's a lot of 'em in prison you see.

Monica Oh!

Martin Take no notice; he's in the last stages of flying dementia.

Chapman Really. Now who is it who's come from Australia? Martin was telling us.

Fiona Jimmy and I have come home for Christmas. First time in thirty years.

Martin (*to Chapman and Monica*) Can I get you some drinks there?

Chapman A small malt if you have one.

Martin We don't have any small ones but I can do you a large one with half taken out.

Monica A small sweet sherry please.

There is a beat. Martin pours drinks for Monica and Chapman during the following; dry sherry for Monica, Bushmills for Chapman

(*To Fiona*) You must have noticed some changes then?

Jimmy There's hardly anything we recognize; anything that isn't knocked down has been boarded up and half the stuff they've put back in its place has been boarded up too.

Fiona The people are still very nice, though; that hasn't changed.

Chapman We found that when we moved here.

Margaret You're not from around here originally, then?

Monica No, we're originally from Surrey, from Guildford. We moved up here for Chapman's work; he was an accountant with Bikermans the sanitaryware manufacturers.

Margaret And did you work?

Monica I was a flower arranger. I still do demonstrations but I work part-time as a Co-ordinator for "Meals on Wheels". I could get more money flower-arranging down south but we get more sightings up here you see. So when Chapman came to retire we just decided to stay up here. It's better for sightings; the air's clearer and there's not so much reflection off the city lights.

Margaret Are you bird-watchers?

Monica and Chapman shake their heads and smile

Martin It's astronomy; you have to have the clear air for that and you don't want the bright lights. There's a feller on the site built himself a lovely observatory in the back garden.

Goff For a fiver.

Martin A tenner and three pints. We had to get the roof off another site.

Chapman No, no. It's nothing at all like that.

Monica It's angels.
Margaret (*flatly*) Angels. Well done, Martin; this beats the drunken paperboys.
Monica We're on the look-out for angels.

In the following sequence, Monica and Chapman are like train spotters reading out a list of their "hits", counting them out on their fingers

Chapman We are constantly alert and on the watch for the manifestation of all kinds of heavenly hosts: Cherubim, Seraphim and Thrones in the first circle ——
Monica — Dominions, Virtues and Powers in the second circle; we haven't seen many of those ——
Chapman — Principalities and Archangels, and then your ordinary common or gardener angels. We've seen quite a few of those.
Monica And Chapman once saw Uriel in Sainsbury's while we were getting some cat-litter. He was hovering over the frozen fish.
Fiona Muriel?
Chapman Uriel, like Ezekiel and Gabriel; he's one of the major archangels.

Goff is showing signs of distress. He mouths the word "Barking" to Martin, who nods

Monica Pardon?
Goff The dog, barking; I thought I heard him.
Monica We don't have a dog any more. The heavenly hosts don't mind cats but they are allergic to dogs. We used to have one. He was a Pomeranian Rottweiler cross called Trixi. (*Beat*) We had him put down when he went for one of the Seraphim.
Fiona How long have you been seeing angels then?
Chapman Ooh, I suppose it must be ten years at least.
Monica We were both abducted ten years ago by aliens. That's when it all began. We're founder members of the North West Abductees Group. Chapman's the treasurer. His accountancy experience came in very handy there, of course.
Helen You were abducted! What happened?
Chapman We were walking Trixi on Blackstone Edge one lovely summer's evening when we heard a noise in the sky — (*he becomes expansive*) like a great vacuum cleaner; this powerful humming filled the air all around us. And suddenly everything took on a strange patina.
Goff (*fairly gobsmacked with it all; dully*) Patina.
Monica Trixi ran off and we looked up into the sky and this great silver saucer-like thing — ship we call it now — came down over us ever so gently and settled down on the rocks close by.

There is a beat; hold this for a while

Chapman And the next thing we knew she was being interfered with and I had a plastic tube on my penis.

Helen Does anybody want a cup of tea?

Goff Can I have a large alcofrolic drink, please? From anybody. Anybody at all. And anything.

Chapman We know now of course that it was only a scout ship that came down and that it took us up to the mother ship. That was where they took our clothes off.

Monica They wanted our eggs and semen to create a super race with their kind.

Martin (*aside*) A super race of accountants and flower arrangers — Holy Saint Patrick and his shamrock Y-fronts.

Monica They have an interplanetary crèche up there. We saw it; it was full of little babies that were half human, half alien, or, as we call them now, knowing better: "angels".

Goff A very very large one, just big and in a glass; no, a bucket.

Martin (*transfixed*) Yes, yes, me too!

Chapman At first we couldn't understand their language; it sounded like squeaks and chirrups.

Goff Squeaks and chirrups.

Margaret I think I'll have a very very large drink too. What about you, Jimmy?

Jimmy is open-mouthed and dazed; he just nods very, very emphatically

Jimmy (*low-volume, low-key, almost zombie-like*) Big, big, oh yes; very, very big.

Margaret What about you, Fiona?

Fiona is open-mouthed and unhearing; she is totally out of it

Monica Once we could understand them it was obvious that they were looking for a certain calibre of person to mate with for their master-race.

Goff Sanitaryware Accountants.

Martin And "Meals on Wheels" Co-ordinators.

Chapman We felt a bit weird at first.

Goff Well, you would do. I mean you go for a walk on Blackstone Edge and the next thing you know a mobile sperm and egg bank has come down and taken a deposit — without a by-your-leave.

Martin No bottle of wine, no flowers, no foreplay, no violins; nothing.

Monica We felt quite distressed at first, then we talked it over and Chapman — his accountancy training has given him a very practical approach to life — "Monica", he said, "if we have been abducted by aliens and sexually tampered with, then it must be part of a cosmic plan. We have been singled out."

Chapman So now we keep a constant look-out for the angels. We're Christians, you see.

Monica Chapman used to be the President of the Christian Accountants Association.

Chapman And we know now that they are God's messengers; true Angels.

Monica And that only when all Mankind has mated with His angels will there be salvation.

Goff gets up, grabs the bottle of Bushmills and swigs as much of it as he can. He shakes his head. None of the others hears his next line

Goff (*to nowhere in particular*) No; they're still here.

Margaret And you still see angels do you?

Chapman Oh, all the time. As well as the cosmic messengers we see all the usual kinds of angels.

Monica The ones with the wings and the haloes like you see in the paintings.

Chapman They were very accurate, some of those old artists, you know. They knew more than we give them credit for.

Martin And you see them all over, then, these angels?

Chapman Oh, yes. (*He nods towards Fiona*) There's one sitting on her shoulder now.

Fiona jumps up and screams hysterically. This sets the dog off

Fiona Aaagh! Get it off, get it off me, Jimmy, get it off!

Jimmy runs over and brushes the angel off

Jimmy (*explaining to the others*) She's funny about stuff like that. She were frightened by a rubber spider when she were little; she can't settle if she sees a daddy-long-legs on the curtains now.

Chapman It's all right, it's gone now.

Monica It knows there's a dog in the house.

Goff Well, now. (*He stands*) Traditionally on Christmas Eve we always have a bit of a sing-song — and traditionally I always begin, so here goes. (*He sings; to the tune "In And Out The Windows"*)

        Oh, the black cat piddled in the white cat's eye
        The white cat said "Gor Blimey"
        The black cat said "I'm sorry, mate,
        I didn't know you were behind me."

(Tune: "The Girl I Left Behind Me")
>   Oh, I love you in your party frock
>   And I love you in your dress
>   I love you in your cardigan
>   And I love you in your vest
>   But the time I love you best of all

(Molto rallentando)
>   Is when you take off your nightie

(Presto)
>   'Cos when the moonlight flits across your tits
>   Jesus Christ Almighty!

There is stunned silence at the end of this

(Turning to Monica and Chapman) Right, your turn; what are you going to give us? Some Pearl Carr and Teddy Johnstone? Elton John and Kiki Dee?

Monica and Chapman stand to leave

Monica Well, I'm sorry — it's been a lovely visit but we have to be going.
Margaret Looking for angels?
Monica And the turkey; I'm going to have to stuff it tonight.
Goff And obviously you'll have to keep the sperm count up in case the aliens need a donation in the night; lots of raw eggs and sea food.
Chapman Well, yes, of course. And though I sense that I am in the presence of unbelievers I must tell you that you never know. You may be chosen next! One of our most notorious scoffers and deriders vanished off the golf course at Middleton last month only to return hours later with shaved genitalia and a case of hiccups that didn't leave him for a fortnight.
Monica He doesn't mock now.
Martin Well, I'd better change me underpants then, I've had these on a week.
Monica The heavenly hosts are against underpants of any kind. They can lower the sperm count. Chapman has been underpants-free since the abduction.
Chapman Ye may sneer. For is it not written, "They shall mock ye in the market place and their words will be as snow that falleth upon the bonfire." I will leave you with the words Ezekiel said to me on our first abduction: "Cast off thy undergarments and nether cloths for yea it is written: Y-fronts are an insult to the majesty of the penis."

Monica and Chapman exit

There is a long beat

Margaret Martin, this is the last time I say this, but if ever again you open my front door to a pair of barking-mad nutters like that, then you are dead, do you understand me? Do you?

Martin Yes. (*He becomes subdued*) But how was I to know our new neighbours are a boy scout short of a jamboree?

Goff You never know what's coming through that front door. Best thing is to let no-one in.

Martin You can't judge by appearances; they looked perfectly normal to me.

Goff That's the way of the world. (*He makes a wide expansive sweep of his arm that includes the audience*) There are more things, Martin, between Heaven and Earth ... There are people out there that get up to all sorts that you and I wouldn't know about. Never judge by appearances. They might look like Mr and Mrs Normal on the outside but on the inside we're looking at Mr and Mrs Fruitcake!

Jimmy (*changing the subject*) You were in fine voice there Goff; give us another one.

Goff Nay, it's somebody else's turn; Helen, what about you?

Helen I'd crack the glass; what about you, Mum?

Margaret Who, me? What about you, Jimmy? You were rock and roll king of the Bolton Locarno once over; give us one of the old songs.

Fiona Do one you can remember all the words to — don't go forgetting them half-way through. Every time we have a barbie he gets fresh and starts a song and can't finish it.

Goff *See-saw Marjorie Daw*; you must know that one, Jimmy. It's got a saw in it.

Margaret (*icily*) Will you shut up.

Goff Give us *See-saw Marjorie Daw* Jimmy.

Jimmy What.

Goff Or *Woodman Spare that Tree*.

Jimmy What's he on about?

Goff Or *I saw Esau Sittin' on the See-saw*.

Jimmy I don't know what you've been drinking, Goff, but you'd better give me some because I don't know what the bloody hell you're on about.

Goff I'm on about a saw, a bloody saw. It was me first saw when I started work and it were a Raper and Wyman; best Sheffield steel, and it were hand cut and it had just been sharpened and somebody not a million miles away borrowed it to saw two foot off his Aunty Whatsit's bloody pigging bloody clothes bloody prop and buggered off to piggin' Australia with it.

Jimmy That was thirty bloody years ago.

Goff A saw is a saw is a saw.

Helen (*to the ceiling, laconically*) Gertrude Stein.

Goff Whether it were thirty years ago or thirty hundred (*he is exasperated. He searches for words. Beat*) million years ago doesn't bloody piggin' matter.

Jimmy (*in confusion*) I can't remember all that way back.

Goff Well, I can.

Jimmy (*light dawning*) Just a minute, just a minute. I remember now. The saw.

Goff The saw! Hallelujah!

Jimmy I gave it back.

Goff You bloody well didn't!

Margaret For God's sake Goff, I'll buy you another one. I'll buy you two bloody saws, I'll buy you a bloody (*she is lost for words*) bucketful of saws.

Jimmy I did — I gave it back.

Goff Not to me, you didn't!

Jimmy I remember now, because I knew what an old woman you were about your tools.

Goff *Old woman* — if I were thirty years younger I'd ——

Martin Hold your horses there, Goff, you're not in your own house now!

Jimmy I gave it to Fiona. I remember it was wrapped up in newspaper and tied up with hairy string and I told her to be careful she didn't catch her leg with it.

Goff Well, where the bloody hell did it go then? Because it never came home!

Fiona I sold it.

Goff You sold it! You sold my Raper and Wyman saw!

Fiona (*in a burst of wild energy*) Yes, I sold it! I sold it to buy a bloody wedding ring! Because he (*she points at Jimmy*) had spent all his money on the tickets to Australia and because you took so much off me in housekeeping that I was walking round in rags half the time and I was four months pregnant and three pounds short of a wedding ring and I didn't want people on the boat to know that we weren't married.

Goff You sold my Raper and Wyman saw to buy a wedding ring.

Fiona Yes.

Goff (*gobsmacked*) That's — that's — that's ... Only a woman would sell a Raper and Wyman saw to buy a wedding ring.

Martin (*quietly*) I would, but then again I always was a romantic fool.

Goff (*ignoring Martin*) Who did you sell it to?

Fiona Stan Ellison.

Goff Stan Ellison! Stan Ellison! He already had me sash cramps; it took me years to get them back too.

Jimmy (*holding his chest*) Oooh ooh ooh aagh.

Fiona Oh my God, it's his angina; now look what you have done!

Jimmy (*in distress*) No, it's not that. Oh my God.

Martin Jesus Mary and Joseph!!

Margaret Trumpton!!

Goff The piggin' dog, the piggin' dog; Christ, I can't breathe.

Fiona (*crying*) It was me wedding ring.
Martin Get out you little bugger.
Fiona Twelve pounds seven and six, that's all it cost — from Brissendens.
Margaret He's under the tree.
Martin Would you come on out of that you smelly little swine!
Fiona It was in the sale.
Helen Dad don't hit him!
Martin I'll wring his bloody neck.
Fiona I'm still wearing it.
Margaret I think I'm going to be sick.
Martin Out, you little bugger.

Martin gets up to shoo the dog out and trips over the Christmas tree lights cable, pulling the tree down

Carol singers begin to sing "Jingle Bells", off

There is a dull explosion, with smoke, from the tree and the stage is plunged into very deep darkness. Simultaneously, all on stage shout at the carol singers

All Bugger off!!

CURTAIN

ACT II

Christmas morning

The Christmas tree, though it has its lights (now working again) and baubles, has shed every single one of its needles. Carols are spouting from the television, which flickers on the set. The tea tray, with nothing on it, is in evidence. Helen sits in her dressing-gown and nightie with a bowl of cereal, her eyes fixed to the TV screen, waiting for the house to wake

Fiona comes in, also in dressing-gown and nightie

Helen (*not looking up*) Morning, happy Christmas. (*She stands to kiss Fiona*) I've just put the kettle on for some more coffee.

Fiona Happy Christmas. (*She gives Helen a peck on the cheek*) I didn't hear anybody else stirring. Jimmy's decided he's got jet lag and he's staying in bed for a bit; he was up till all hours with Martin and Goff. I think it's more likely Guinness-and-whisky lag. But he'd never admit to that. Does your dad normally drink that much?

Helen He doesn't actually. He just likes to let his hair down and have a good time on special occasions.

Fiona Like weddings and Christmas and funerals.

Helen No. Like Monday, Tuesday, Wednesday, Thursday. He's the last of the Good Time Charlies. They broke the mould when they made him. It's like Uncle Goff. You don't get many of them to the pound.

Fiona I'd forgotten quite what he can be like. I remember him driving Mum mad with his antics. Like when he took his motorbike apart in the kitchen and we had to climb over bits of chain and pistons for three whole months while he waited for somebody at work to turn him a new whatsit. I used to think that everybody in the world had the petrol tank off a Royal Enfield permanently on the sideboard. What's that you're watching?

Helen Some clapped-out superstar going to Africa for charity being condescending to the natives for a couple of days before flying back to his mansion in Berkshire. That kind of thing.

Fiona Bit cynical, isn't it?

Helen Well, I'm a teacher; what do you expect?

Fiona How long have you been teaching now?

Helen Ten years.

Fiona Where are you at? Knaresborough, isn't it?

Helen Yes, Knaresborough: proof that God had a sense of humour; Yorkshire's answer to Bognor Regis. Knaresborough: where they stand the dead up in bus queues.

Fiona It's posh, isn't it, Knaresborough? I remember going there when we were kids at school. "Mother Shipton's Well" we shouted at the driver of the coach and he said, "I didn't know she'd been ill". We thought it was dead funny but apparently he said that to all the kids, 'cos when we got back to school the class above us already knew it. (*A long beat*) It's funny coming back; there's so many memories. Still, you must like it to stick it out.

Helen It has its moments. The school I teach in isn't particularly rough — by which I mean that we only get two teachers a year put in hospital — but I've had a squash racquet thrown at me for telling a lad off, my car windscreen put in for sending somebody to the head for carrying a knife and I've had my tits felt twice by thirteen-year-old boys. The chemistry teacher flipped last term and turned a fire extinguisher on two kids.

Fiona Why, for God's sake?

Helen They were advancing towards him with Bunsen burners.

Fiona That's terrible. I read that things were a bit bad in the papers that Jimmy used to get sent over but I'd no idea they were that bad.

Helen They don't want teachers any more, you've got to be a cross between an ex-SAS bouncer and a childminder. What they should do is take all the teachers and Winnie-the-Pooh, out into the school yard, stand them all up against the wall and machine gun the lot of them.

Fiona Why Winnie-the-Pooh?

Helen You see: nobody gives a chuff about the teachers. (*Beat*) But it does have its rewards. I get to look after the wildlife over the holidays.

Fiona What wildlife?

Helen (*indicating the aquarium*) The stick insects.

Fiona Is that what's in there? I thought it was maybe a lizard or something.

Helen It's the Head's idea: "Bringing a bit of the green world into the classroom," he calls it. (*She moves to the aquarium and feeds the stick insects*) It was either that or the hamster and it's a good job I chose these because the cats would have had the hamster. There's twelve of them in there but you can't see them because they look just like the twigs.

Fiona You all seem to be on edge about these cats — what are they like?

Helen Monsters. Our Kathy is out all day working so they have the place to themselves. Then when she comes home she ruins them to compensate. So they're spoilt rotten. She gives them smoked salmon and they have their own sheepskin beds. They hate it up here; they think the North's dead rough. Last time they came here the ginger tom from next door battered the pair of them so she used to leave them in a cattery after that, but they're all full in London. So when she knew she was bringing them up North again she bought them two little suits of armour, a flat 'at apiece and some aerosol tripe-scented whippet repellant.

Fiona (*humourlessly*) That's nice. (*Beat*) What time's Kathy coming?

Helen Well, she should be here soon. They set off early so they could be here to open the presents with everybody. That's why me mum told us not to open them last night; she's a great stickler for traditions. She still makes me a stocking up with an orange and some nuts in it and a few bits and pieces.

Fiona What does she do then, your Kath? It was something to do with art the last time your mother mentioned anything.

Helen She runs a gallery down in London. It's all very modern and I don't understand it. We used to have rows about it; now we agree to disagree.

Fiona She's bringing a boyfriend, your Kath; have you met him?

Helen No, but if it's anything like the usual ones she drags up here it will be interesting.

Goff enters with another bag of greens from his allotment. He looks very smart in a suit with a cardigan et cetera, and his shoes are polished, but the effect is rather spoilt by a red baseball cap with reindeer horns on it. He is a bit squiffy

Goff Happy Christmas and a Merry New Year to all here. (*He kisses Fiona*) Happy Christmas, love. (*He kisses Helen*) Happy Christmas to my favourite second niece or second cousin or whatever it is.

Helen Been to Mass?

Goff Yes. Canon O'Connor, or as I now call him, Speedy O'Gonzales. He were merely a blur on that altar this morning. The altar boys were dizzy trying to keep up with him. Some of them altar boys are girls by the way now. Anyroad up it were all done and dusted in thirty-seven minutes. I'm going to stop putting so much on the plate if we're only going to get half a show. He waited outside to shake everybody's hands after Mass and wish them all a happy Christmas. Then he invited me in to the presbytery for something to warm me up.

Helen It smells like you've been drinking rocket fuel — what is it?

Fiona I'll get the coffee. (*She goes into the kitchen*)

Goff It's potato water. Special stuff. We go back a long way me and Canon O'Connor. I knew him when he had a bike and used to give t' longest penances in Lancashire. Church used to be full wi' people doin' hundreds of "Our Fathers", "Hail Marys" and "Glory Bes". There all night, mumblin' away. Hundreds of 'em. Till the publicans complained to the bishop that they were losing business. That stopped it. (*He produces a huge full lemonade bottle and puts it on the table*) Potheen, th' Irish moonshine; he gets it off a lad from Sligo lives in the hills over Blackburn way. He has a still up there on a pig farm. The police think he's boilin' pig swill up but he makes the best stuff you'll ever taste. I got your dad a bottle off Canon O'Connor. Liquid dynamite. Ten quid and there must be more than two pints in there. Best stuff there is, that. (*He shows the others the contents of his bag*) Now then, look at them, that's what I call sprouts: grown on nowt but muck. None of your hydroponics and chemical fertilizers in this lot, just good honest (*he savours the word*) dung. Untouched by ICI. That's why the sperm count is going down, you know.

Fiona (*through the hatch*) Dad!

Goff It's true. Chemicals in food and tight underpants. And the other thing is the pill. Women are on the pill and they pee out ostrichgen, eastergen, whatever, and it gets in the reservoirs and men drink it and the sperm count goes down.

Fiona (*returning*) Dad, it's Christmas Day!

Goff Christmas Day or not, the sperm count's going down. (*Beat*) It'll be no good havin' a redeemer when there's nobody left to redeem. And it's tight underpants that's doing it. (*He starts unpacking the greens and waves a huge cucumber about unconsciously*) There was never any bother in the old days when yer tackle used to just hang loose. It was all you could manage not to get pregnant, then. Now they're having to have babies in test tubes. Like them nutters from down the crescent with their spaceships and their angels. In vitreous fertilisation. Vitreous; that was what they did to gas boilers in th' old days! Cloning! What was wrong with th' old-fashioned way — what was wrong with that eh? (*He produces a couple of small but impressive turnips from the bag. The visual result, with the cucumber, is as you might expect*) Test-tube babies! What's wrong wi' blokes nowadays? Have they forgot what to do? They aren't mekin' 'em like they used to, that's the trouble. Tight underpants and dioxins. They don't need the bomb any more, we're wipin' ourselves out. (*He notices the tree and lets the vegetables droop*) Bloody Hell! That looks sad. Your mam'll go mad. Are they up yet?

Helen Up and out, they've gone to Mass. They've gone to the Holy Name again. (*To Fiona, explaining*) They still say the Mass in Latin there.

Goff I used to like the Latin. They used to have bingo every Friday at the Holy Name Catholic Club and they used to call out the numbers in Latin so the Protestants couldn't win. (*He intones*) "Key of the door, ex ex eye; two fat ladies vee eye eye eye," and if you had a full card you shouted "Domus domus!"

Fiona They didn't, did they? That's cruel!

Helen Goff, that's an old one; you used to say that when I was a kid.

Goff I thought you'd have forgotten. I'll have to get a new scriptwriter. Anyway I don't like all this modern comedy, all this effin' and jeffin'. Ted

Ray were modern enough for me. Eeeh, another Christmas. Where does it all go? It hardly seems five minutes since the last one. *(To Fiona)* And when I think back it hardly seems ten minutes since I were creeping upstairs with your pillow case full of presents. Now look at you, with kids of your own. *(Beat)* Eeh, another Christmas, another year nearer the grave. We're just in God's waiting room, that's all, shuffling along minute by minute towards the big drop. *(A long beat; then, suddenly and brightly)* Anyway, bugger it! "All good things must come to an end," as the nun said when she bit the bum off the sugar elephant and "We're not dead yet," said Tutankhamun. What time's herself and Picasso getting here?

Helen Goff!

Fiona Picasso! What's he talking about?

Helen Our Kathy's friend is something to do with the arts and as far as Goff is concerned that means he is a pretentious ponce.

Goff Most of them are. Making a pile of bricks and calling it art. Art my backside.

Fiona Oh. Well, that'll be nice. We know an artist in Adelaide. He paints the bush a lot.

Goff Just the one?

Fiona What?

Goff Bush. He just paints this bush, does he? Outside his door; goes out with a can of paint and slaps it on?

Fiona Oh, I get it.

Goff You're even slower than you were. It must be walking upside-down for thirty years — the blood's all settled in your head.

The doorbell rings

Helen I wonder if it's our Kath?

Helen exits to the front door

(Off) Where's your key?

Margaret and Martin enter with Helen

Margaret *(as they enter)* Ask that idiot.
Martin Merry Christmas to all here from the idiot.

There are kisses all round

Margaret Well honestly — you wouldn't believe it.
Martin Francie Walsh was locked out of his car so I tried to see if I could

open it with my keys and they fell out of me hand, it was that cold. I dropped them and they fell down the flamin' grid.

Margaret The whole bloody lot of them — house keys, work keys, car keys, the lot. Barney Sullivan brought us home. Christmas morning and your father's in the gutter flat out in his best suit down a grid with a coat hanger we've borrowed from the presbytery. And they're all going in to eleven o'clock Mass. I bet they all thought he was drunk, lying down flat out and me grinning at them all like a fool, as though that's what you did on Christmas morning, lie in the gutter in your best suit. He gets worse, showing us up like that.

Helen Did you find them?

Margaret Did we 'eck as like. They're still stuck down there. The coat hanger wasn't long enough. He wants to get the corporation out. I said, "On Christmas Day!! You'll be lucky. You can't get 'em out at the best of times — never mind Christmas Day!" Ooh, my head, it's banging fit to burst; I'll have to have a paracetamol before I do anything else! Have you checked the turkey?

Helen I looked before; it's lying in a bed of spuds with a bacon brassiere on. It's doing fine for something that was running round in the sunshine last week.

Margaret Don't start your vegetarian rubbish now, I'm not in the mood. I've told you, my girl, everybody's getting what they're given and they can leave what they don't want. Well, I've just time for a cup of tea before the onslaught. I don't suppose Kathy phoned.

Helen She phoned from Keele services. It must have been three hours ago.

Martin Three hours. It shouldn't take them three hours from Keele, not unless they're goin' by Helsinki. They should have been here an hour ago!

Margaret I hope nothing's happened. There's always terrible accidents on Christmas Day and my stars said there would be trouble coming from travellers.

Goff Stop panicking; she'll be here when she's here.

Helen With the cats.

Margaret Well, we'll just have to keep them and the dog apart, that's all. Now where's me pinny? Put the kettle on, love.

Fiona It's on already; it's been on all morning.

Martin Could I tempt you to partake of a small libation, Goff?

Goff Only if you will be partaking of one yourself, my good fellow.

Martin Does the Pope crap on a duck in the woods? Most certainly.

Goff Then fall to, my good man.

Martin And remember: you're not drunk so long as you can lie on the floor without holding on.

Margaret (*ignoring all this*) Martin, hurry up and get us all a drink and I'll not mention the keys again.

Helen I'd better get dressed.

Jimmy enters in his pyjamas and dressing-gown looking totally dishevelled

Fiona Oh, here he is, Australia's answer to Robert Redford. Good-afternoon, Jimmy.

Jimmy What time is it?

Helen Twenty-three minutes past eleven — and a half; but who's counting?

Margaret You're just in time for a drink. What would you like?

Goff Raw egg with a dash of Worcester sauce? Lightly boiled aspirin? Monkey brains on toast?

Jimmy (*with a brave face*) I don't feel so bad actually.

Goff Well, you look like somebody who's gone ten rounds with a mincer and lost. If you were a horse I'd have you put down.

Jimmy Thanks. Happy Christmas, everybody, by the way.

All Happy Christmas.

The doorbell rings and the dog goes mad

Jimmy (*holding his head*) It's got a bloody loud bark, that dog.

Helen I'll get it.

Helen exits to the front door

Hiyaa! What's up? Oh!

Margaret (*to Fiona*) It's our Kathy —— (*She calls into the hall*) What's up?

Kathy runs in carrying the cat baskets

Quick, get me somewhere to put these. Quick! Quick! Hallo everybody. Hi! Hi! Mmm mmm. (*She does quick Sloaney kisses all round*) Quelle disastre! I mean, really — *quelle disastre.*

Crispin enters, walking like Frankenstein's monster

The family react to Crispin, gagging as if there is a bad smell coming from him

This is Crispin, everybody; I'll introduce you all properly in a minute.

Martin (*putting out his hand*) You're very welcome.

Crispin I can't shake your hand I'm afraid. I'm covered from head to foot in a fine patina of cat doo doo.

Goff Patina; I must look that word up.

Margaret What's happened?

Kathy Well, you know how they hate travelling, particularly Tarantino. I mean Jarman's never been exactly comfortable with the car but Tarantino is positively schizoid! Well, they were worse than ever this time. They started pooing as soon as we left London and haven't stopped for four-and-a half-hours. *Quelle* nightmare! I mean ... I mean ... well, they've been pooing solid — well, not *solid*, you know what I mean — without stopping. For nearly six hours. The inside of his car is covered in it. He's got some on him too. I was sat on the back seat with their baskets so it missed me. They got their little botties up against the bars of the cage and resprayed the interior of his BMW. And it's only three days old.

Crispin Four hundred miles on the clock and covered in cat doo doo.

Goff A patina.

Kathy Let's get them in the bathroom and get them cleaned up. (*An afterthought*) Crispin, there's another bathroom and toilet in Mum and Dad's bedroom, yeah? You can get yourself sorted out there.

Helen I'll give you a hand, then I'll get changed.

Kathy goes off with Helen to sort the cats out. Crispin follows

Margaret Martin, give me a quick drink.

Fiona I'd better get changed too or I'll be in my nightie all day. I'll give you a hand in a minute, Peggy.

Fiona exits

Goff pours a glass of potheen for Margaret

Goff Here get your laughing tackle round this.

Margaret Cheers. (*She knocks the potheen back in one and loses her voice immediately*)

For a while nobody notices Margaret's distress

Goff (*to Martin*) I got a bottle of the old stuff for you off Canon O'Connor. Happy Christmas.

Martin (*smelling the potheen*) Cripes, that'd shave the donkey! Lemonade — another miracle! But I think it's a bit too early for the bottled kryptonite.

Margaret (*giving out hoarse whispers and frantically flapping her hands, sitting down with a bump on the settee*) Ash hashas warra shassas swarra.

Martin What?

Margaret Hashas warra shassas swarra.

Goff I thought it were quite mellow, smooth almost.

Martin You could drink sulphuric acid and it wouldn't bother you. (*To Margaret*) What's up?

Margaret points towards the kitchen. The dog starts barking

Margaret (*faintly*) Water.

Martin What? (*To the dog*) Shut up, you little bugger.

Margaret (*fainter*) Water.

Martin I can't hear a word yer sayin'.

Margaret (*basso profundo; loudly*) WATER, YOU PILLOCK!

Martin goes into the kitchen

Fiona enters; she has changed out of her night things

Fiona They've sorted the cats out; they're just drying them with a hair dryer.

Martin (*coming back in with a glass of water*) A friggin' hair dryer! Them cats get better looked after than I do!

Fiona They seem nice cats.

Goff Want another one, Margaret?

Margaret I do not. It was like drinking hot razor blades. Me wobbs have gone all kneely.

Martin You what?

Margaret Me. (*She gets flustered and points at her knees*) Me knees, I mean — they've gone whatsit.

Kathy enters

Kathy Well, that's better. Happy Christmas everybody. Hallo Fiona, Jimmy; how was your trip?

Fiona It seems a lifetime ago since we left doesn't it, Jimmy.

Kathy Wow! Wicked! A lifetime, yeah!

Jimmy It's good to be back. You weren't even born when we left.

Jimmy shakes hands with everyone

Kathy Right! Yeah! I got born since though, didn't I? You mustn't take too much notice of what I say for a while; I smoked a big spliff on the way, yeah? The cats and everything, yeah. It was just too much. I'll introduce you to Crispin in a minute, OK? Right now I need an industrial strength glass of bubbly.

Helen comes in from the kitchen with a bottle of champagne and a bucket of ice

Helen Time for the champagne and the presents.
Margaret Good girl.

There is a sudden burst of barking and meowing and hissing, off, tokens of a massive row between the dog and the cats. The dog yelps as well, obviously not getting all his own way

Helen (*dashing towards the exit*) Trumpton!

Helen exits

Kathy (*dashing towards the exit*) Oh my God, the cats!

Kathy exits

Crispin enters, drenched in water

Crispin I am very sorry but one of the taps in the bathroom came off in my hand! There's water everywhere but I managed to stop it by jamming a cake of soap on it.
Margaret (*to Martin*) You and your five-pound bloody taps. (*To Crispin*) I am sorry, Crispin, please sit down and have a drink — I'll get up as soon as I can stand up.

Crispin sits down. Nobody gives him a drink; in fact nobody takes much notice of him throughout the following

(*To Martin*) Well, don't stand there gawpin' — go and fix it.

The following speech has a background of yapping and hissing, off, accompanied by the girls' shouts of "Trumpton", "Tarantino" and "Jarman"

Goff Never let a joiner near plumbing. Never let them anywhere near it. They're all right wi' wood and nails but when it comes to pipes and water — well, they watch a bloke doing it once and think they can do it but it's every man to his trade ——
Martin Would you ever shut up you old bollix.

Martin runs off

Jimmy I'll give you a hand, Martin; then I'd better get changed too.

Kathy enters

Kathy The cats are on the pelmet spitting at the dog and won't come down.
God, somebody give me a drink, perleese!

Helen enters

Helen And the dog has got half his ear ripped off.
Kathy Don't exaggerate, it's only a teeny scratch.
Helen Well, it's pouring in blood! It's all over the kitchen floor.
Kathy That's because there's more blood vessels in the ear. Anyway it
shouldn't have had a go at Jarman and Tarantino. They're not used to dogs.
I thought you were putting him in kennels!
Helen We thought you were putting them in a cattery.
Margaret Don't you two start as well! My nerves won't stand it!

Martin enters

Martin I'll have to turn the water off.
Margaret On Christmas Day! You're going to turn the water off on
Christmas Day? I've got the dinner to cook yet!
Martin It'll only be for half an hour while I get the tap back on.

Martin exits

Margaret *(shocked — as though she's having a heart attack)* Oh! Oh! Oh!
Kathy What's the matter now? This place is too much; it's becoming a mad
house it really is.
Helen Mother! Mother! Your blood pressure.
Kathy I've got to say Crispin that this is typical of my family; dysfunctional
or what?
Margaret The tree! The tree. Last night it was covered in needles and now
there's not a single one left!
Helen Godot.
Kathy What?
Margaret That — that man! I'll swing for him! Five pound taps! Five pound
Christmas trees!

Martin enters

Martin I've sorted it. The thread was crossed that was all. Simple job; I'll just
give it a couple of turns wit' the stiltson and a bit of PFTE and the job's a
good-un.

There is a long silence during which Margaret stares murderously at Martin.
The silence should be sustained as long as possible, even to the extent that
we suspect the actors have dried

Crispin I do hope you are all having a good Christmas. It's so nice to have the family home for Christmas, isn't it?

Margaret (*gibbering because of her nerves and the potheen*) Oh, yes, it's marvellous. (*She gets up and pours herself another potheen inadvertently*) Will you have a drink?

Crispin In a moment. I wondered, could I borrow a shirt and some slacks perhaps until these can be dried? My change of clothing was hanging up in the back of the car. I'm afraid the cats have covered that in doo doo as well.

Goff Are they special cats, these of yours, then, Kath?

Kathy No why?

Goff Well, yours do doo doos — our cat used to shite.

Margaret (*to Crispin*) Of course. (*To Goff*) And you: shut your cakehole, you! (*She downs the drink in one; this time it has no effect on her whatsoever*)

Kathy Cakehole, wow, cakehole! Nobody says that nowadays; how quaint.

Fiona Does anybody mind if I help myself to lemonade? I've got a throat like a kangaroo's bottom. (*Receiving no answer, she pours herself a large potheen and downs it in one. She goes into immediate catatonia, locked solid with the glass in her hand*)

Martin I'll just fix the tap. It'll be good as new. Two minutes. No problem.

Martin exits

Margaret It shouldn't have come off in the first place!

Crispin I didn't pull it hard, you know. I turned it on and when I tried to turn it off it came away in my hand, just snapped off. I don't think it was fixed on properly.

Margaret Like a lot of things in this house; like his (*she points upwards in the general direction of the absent Martin*) piggin' head. Now let's get you some clothes. I'll find you some of Martin's, but I don't know what we can do about that nice jacket of yours; we'll have to get it dry-cleaned.

Crispin and Margaret exit during the following

Crispin They won't be open on Christmas Day.

Margaret (*not listening*) No, that's right. It must be lovely in Basildon. I've never been to Basildon. Is it anywhere near Skegness? We went there once on our holidays — it rained for a fortnight.

Kathy (*pointing at the sprouts*) They look good. Are they yours?

Goff What! Oh ay, they're just about the best I've grown. I've had some good
dung this year. There was a circus in Jubilee Park and me and Eric met the
elephant keeper in the *Cloggers*. A couple of pints or three and the next
thing you know we've got three ton of elephant turds dumped on the
allotment. (*He picks up two of the sprouts and shows them*) Here, what do
you have if you have two little green balls in your hand? Don't know? The
undivided attention of a leprechaun. (*He laughs*) The undivided attention
of a leprechaun.
Kathy I don't get it.
Goff Never mind; I'll draw you a diagram.

They are suddenly conscious of Fiona

Goff Are you all right, love?

*Fiona picks up the tea-tray and uses it as a "wobble board" for a tone-deaf
performance of the first few lines of "Sun Arise" à la Rolf Harris*

The others look puzzled

Curtain

Scene 2

The same day. Later

*Martin, Goff, Margaret, Kathy, Crispin, Fiona and Jimmy are onstage.
Martin and Jimmy are handing round glasses of champagne. Helen and
Kathy are dragging out presents from under the tree. Crispin is wearing some
of Martin's clothes, which are several sizes wrong for him*

Helen Right. Now we usually take it in turns to open the presents so we'll
start with Crispin because he's the guest. (*She picks up a long, thin package
and reads the label*) Here's one from Fiona and Jimmy for Crispin. Happy
Christmas. (*She hands Crispin the package*)
Crispin Well, thank you — this is very nice, and very unexpected.
Fiona Well, we didn't know you were coming until yesterday so it's nothing
very special.

Crispin unwraps the present. It is a tie

Helen Now, Fiona. (*She hands Fiona a present*)

Fiona (*reading the label*) It's from Margaret and Martin. Ooh, it's lovely. (*She unwraps the present; it is a sweater and totally wrong for her since she is all flounce and frills and the sweater is very "Earth Mother"*) It's made by Gandalf's workshop, it says here, " ... from unbleached un-chemically-treated wool from the friendly backs of sheep that live freely on the hills of mid-Wales eating only organic grass. Gandalf and his Hobbit helpers send you greetings." Very nice. Thank you.

Kathy Jimmy. (*She hands him a present*)

Jimmy It's a shame to destroy the wrapping paper, it's wrapped so nice. (*He opens the present; it is a sweater identical to Fiona's*) Oh, that's smashing. It matches Fiona's perfectly. What's that on the front?

Margaret It's a dragon.

Goff You got it wrong: he didn't say he wanted one dragon on the front, he wanted one draggin' on the floor — heh heh heh ...

Everyone stares at Goff

Goff goes into the kitchen

Margaret Eh?

Martin I know what he means. And Christmas Day is not the time for it.

Margaret I'm glad you like them. Me and Helen were at a craft fair and we saw them on this stall full of sweaters. "Knit Picking" it was called. Knit spelt K.N.I.T.. Helen said you'd like them.

Goff comes back with some nibbles and starts handing them round

Helen Mum. (*She hands Margaret her present*)

Margaret (*reading*) "From Kathy and Helen to Mum with love." (*She opens the parcel; it contains a black lace slip and matching bra and pants*) Oh it's lovely. (*She holds up the underwear*)

Martin Very nice, but they'll be bad for me heart.

Margaret Martin, they're nowhere near your size anyway.

Helen (*to Martin, handing him a parcel*) Dad. This is from me and Kathy.

Martin It's big and it's heavy but it doesn't rattle.

Goff As the nun said to the Archbishop — heh heh — as the nun said to the Archbishop.

Martin Would you ever shut up? And are you going to take that daft cap off or are you going to wear it all day?

Goff It's Christmas, season of peace on earth and goodwill to all men, especially me. (*He carries on handing round the nibbles during the following*)

Martin (*opening his parcel and reading*) "*The Reader's Digest Do-It-Yourself Manual*. A thousand and one projects for the handyman." It's even got plans for a loft conversion: "Turn that spare space into an office/den/hi-fi room." Well, there you go. That's next year's project sorted out.

Margaret Oh, my godfathers — more mess.

Kathy (*handing Goff a parcel*) Goff.

Goff (*reading*) "For Great Uncle Goff from Kathy and Helen." It's small, hard and rattles a bit, as the Archbishop said to the nun. (*He opens the parcel*) A gardener's diary, a tin of Uncle Joe's Mint Balls and the book of "The World's Worst Jokes". Very nice. Thank you both very much.

Kathy Our turn. (*She hands a present to Helen*) This is from Mum and Dad for Helen.

Helen (*opening the parcel to reveal a duvet jacket*) Ooh, just what I wanted. That's lovely. That'll keep me nice and warm. That'll be great for playground duty when it's cold.

Kathy (*opening a present*) Mine from Crispin. (*She brings out a brooch and chain and a sweater*) Ooh, Crispin, that is lovely —— (*she gives him a kiss*) — but you shouldn't have.

The others admire her presents

Crispin Why not?

Kathy Well ... well, it's just that ... I only got you a little present. (*She gives him a present*)

Crispin But it's the thought that counts surely. (*He opens the present; it is a pair of socks and two ties*)

Goff gets up again and hands the nibbles round

Helen There's another one here from Mum and Dad for Crispin.

Crispin So many presents. (*He opens his parcel; it is another tie*) Shouldn't somebody else open theirs?

Martin I want to open one of mine. What about me?

Margaret He's like a big kid, like a big soft kid.

Helen Here you are. It's from Mum to you. (*She reads the label*)
>   "To my darling darling Martin
>   Who crossed the Irish Sea —
>   Irish eyes are always smiling
>   My Rose of Tralee."

Tralee! Me Dad's from Dublin!

Margaret I know, but it doesn't rhyme with sea.

Goff Bubblin' does; you could have written something about bubbling. Like "as black as Guinness bubbling".

Margaret Bloody critics — they're all the piggin' same. Never do anythin' but always tellin' others how it should be done! What do you know about writing? The last thing you wrote was a letter to the *Chronicle* about dog mess on the bowling green.

Goff Well, it was me best jack. It ruined the game for me, that did.

Martin (*opening his parcel; it contains a pair of boxer shorts which he holds up*) Boxer shorts! I only wear Y-Fronts, you know that!

Margaret Well, you can start wearin' them. I read that Y-Fronts are bad for you. They can give you strictures.

Goff It's tight underpants what's lowering the sperm count. Keep wearing them Y-Fronts and the angels won't be looking for you on Blackstone Edge.

Crispin Sorry? Sorry, I missed that one?

Goff It's very post-Post-Modern.

Kathy (*reading a label*) "For My Darling Peggy from your darling Martin." It's a big one, Mother.

Everyone except Crispin and Goff says the next line, pre-empting Goff

All As the Archbishop said to the nun.

Margaret (*opening the parcel, revealing a long and very smart dress*) It's lovely Martin. I'll go and try it on.

Margaret exits with the dress

Goff Fiver off the site?

Martin Up a bit.

Goff Feller on the mixer makes 'em, does he?

Martin His daughter does. She's got her own dress shop. I swapped him three baths and six bags of cement for it.

Helen (*picking up a present; a small box so we know it isn't a tie*) Here, Crispin, this is from me. (*She reads the label*) "For Crispin". (*She hands over the present*)

Crispin takes a while to unwrap the present; there is time for some business here. The gift is revealed to be a bow tie

Crispin It is very lovely, Helen; thank you.

Goff Go out a lot do you, Crispin?

Crispin I like ties, really I do.

Goff It's a good job 'cos that's what I've got you an' all. (*He hands Crispin a present*)

Kathy (*reading a label*) "For Helen from Kathy and Crispin." (*She hands Helen the present, a very odd-looking parcel*)

Helen Ooh, thanks. (*She starts unwrapping the parcel*)

Crispin We had oodles of trouble wrapping it.

Kathy Crispin suggested bin liners in the end; he said it would look very post-punk.

Helen reveals a very ugly, very big, minimalist steel "industrial" lamp, the kind of thing that would look well in a Soho loft but totally out of keeping with Helen's Earth-Motherish image

Helen (*unconvincingly*) That's lovely.

Goff Well, t' dog'll have somewhere to pee, anyroad.

Helen It's lovely, thank you both. (*She kisses Kathy and Crispin*) This is for you from me. (*She hands Kathy a minute parcel*)

Kathy Oh lovely. (*She opens a the parcel, revealing a brooch*) Oooh, a brooch. What are these marks on it?

Helen Your name in runes.

Kathy (*unconvincingly*) Ooh, wow.

Helen And this is for you as well. *(She hands Kathy another parcel)*

Kathy Wow, two presents. (*She rips the present open*) A bottle of Ylang Ylang aromatherapy bath oil and a CD of North American tribal chants sung to the backing of whale songs. (*Again unconvincingly*) Oh, that's lovely, thank you. (*She kisses Helen*)

Goff (*handing Kathy a present*) Here you are Kathy — from Mum and Dad.

Kathy (*opening the parcel to reveal a dressing-gown and slippers — very fluffy and pink and very much not the kind of thing she would ever wear*) Wicked! Wow! (*She stands and holds them against herself to show them off*)

Margaret returns

Margaret That'll keep you warm in that flat when you get up in the morning. It was freezing last time we were down there, so I said to your dad, "I'm getting her something warm and practical for Christmas this year. Never mind book tokens; we'll get her something that she can use."

Kathy Wicked! I'll put some curlers in and go round frightening the neighbours.

Crispin Well, I don't know about the neighbours, it will certainly terrify me, waking up to that in the morning! Ha ha ha.

There is a long silence as it occurs to everybody that Kathy and Crispin are actually an item

Helen (*holding out a long, thin parcel to Goff*) Here you are, Goff — from Jimmy and Fiona . It says here: "Up from down under."

Martin I'm just going to check that tap isn't dripping.

Martin exits

Kathy eats some nibbles during the following

Goff Ta very muchness, love. (*He takes the parcel and opens it slowly, we are not to know what it is until the last piece of paper falls off*) It looks like another tie, Crispin. It's long and thin as the choirboy said to the vicar (*the parcel, of course, contains a saw*) — bloody hellfire! Well! Thank you .. I mean ... that's ... well, I'll go to the foot of our stairs. It's nice and sharp.

Fiona I got Helen to run me round to B & Q — it's a good job there was late shopping.

Goff (*reading the label on the saw*) Sandvik — I suppose it's German. Raper and Wyman went out of business years ago. They don't do them with proper ash handles any more, do they? Nothing's the same nowadays.

Fiona These are lovely nibbles, Margaret. Where did you get them?

Margaret I don't know if I did get them. I bought some Speedy Gonzales Tacos and some Kettle Crisps. I don't remember buying these. Where did you get them, Goff?

Goff They were in a box on the side with some of the stuff that Kathy bought. Smoked Salmon Nibblers or something.

Kathy (*spitting them out*) Cat food, cat food; you've given us all bloody cat food.

Goff Cat food comes in a tin!

Kathy Not the kind that Jarman and Tarantino have; it's dry.

Goff Well, that's bloody daft!

Kathy But it has a cat on the packet.

Goff So! Frosties have a tiger on t' packet. You don't see tigers in t' jungle sittin' down to a bowl of Frosties.

Margaret He's mad — barking mad.

They are all in various degrees of confusion and distress, drinking Coke to get rid of the cat food taste et cetera

Martin sticks his head through the hatch

Martin (*to Helen*) Did you take the turkey out of the oven?
Helen I took it out to let it cool down; why?
Martin You left it in the porch with the door open, didn't you?
Helen The kitchen was full of steam. Why, what's up?
Martin The turkey's up, that's what! Up the garden path! The bloody dog's just buggered off wit' the turkey, draggin' it be the bloody leg. The last thing I saw it was off down the bloody avenue with it. It'll be a tin of ham

with holly on it for Christmas dinner now.

Margaret (*collapsing on to the settee again and at the end of all of her tethers*) Christmas! Christmas! (*She thinks hard for the worst swear word she can find*) Buggering bloody sod Christmas!

Black-out

SCENE 3

It is late afternoon / early evening

The Lights come up. Martin, Margaret, Kathy, Crispin, Fiona, Jimmy and Goff are all onstage, variously strewn about the room. Dinner is over and everybody is quite merry, flushed and finished off with paper hats

Goff Well, Margaret you surpassed yourself. That was a lovely dinner that; lovely dinner. I've had good 'uns before but that were the best; lovely, that were.

Martin Considering the bloody turkey only had one leg.

Goff If the dog hadn't got it jammed between the manikin *pis* and the fishing garden gnomes up at Cap de Lunatics we'd have had nowt; it would have had the whole bloody thing away. Anyroad up, we didn't fall out over the leg.

Martin No, because you got it.

Goff Well, that's because I'm th'eldest. It's a mark of respect.

Helen What about a game?

Fiona Oooh, great let's play some games.

Crispin Does anybody play bridge?

Everyone looks at Crispin

All (*variously*) No. No. Sorry. No, not really, *et cetera.*

Crispin Chess?

Helen Well, I can play but I'm no good. And I don't think we've got a chessboard any more, have we, Mum?

Margaret Not since your father used it to fix Canon O'Connor's melodeon.

Goff We could have a game of doms.

Helen You always cheat.

Goff How can you cheat at doms?

Martin Knocking when you can go and hanging back till you get a run and catch everybody else out, that's how!

Goff We were only playin' for matchsticks!

Martin That's not the point.

There is a long long silence until again we almost believe the actors have dried

Margaret We've got Spillikins.
Kathy Charades.
Goff We always fall out if we play that.
Helen That's because you cheat.
Goff How can you cheat at charades?
Helen *You* can.
Jimmy Go on, I haven't played charades in years.
Goff Right: men versus women.
Crispin I don't believe I've ever played this game.
Kathy Oh, Crispin! You don't mean you've never played charades! What did you do in your spare time at public school?
Crispin Well, those of us who weren't having affairs with the new boys used to read or go for walks. I played bridge and Monopoly. And I can play Scrabble.
Kathy I can't believe you've never played charades.
Martin They don't do stuff like that in Basildon. They get the poor people to do it for them.
Margaret I'll do you in a minute. Don't worry, Crispin love, you'll soon pick it up.
Helen You just have to act out a book or a play or a film or TV show or song title.
Goff It's dead easy, dead easy; you'll soon pick it up. (*He fetches a pen and a piece of paper and scribbles a note*) Kathy — you go first for t'lasses. (*He gives Kathy the note*)
Kathy (*looking at the paper*) Cripes! Wow! Wicked! What is it?
Goff It's a book. (*He takes the note from Kathy and shows it to the men*)

The men smile knowingly

Martin It's a book right enough.
Goff You've got three minutes starting now.
Kathy (*making the sign to indicate a book*) Mmmm.
Margaret We already know it's a book.
Kathy (*stumped*) Mmmm.
Helen Give us the first word.
Jimmy No clues, just mime it.

Kathy mimes "t" for "the"

Fiona
Helen   } (*together*) The! The! The!
Margaret
Goff Bloody brilliant.
Margaret Shut up, you!

Helen Next word.

Kathy makes the "sounds like" sign

Margaret Sounds like.

Kathy mimes a flying insect

Helen Flying.
Fiona Bird.
Margaret Fly — sounds like fly.

Kathy makes a jabbing sign in the air

Helen Sword — stab.
Margaret What's she doing?
Fiona Sounds like "flying stab".

Kathy shakes her head, flaps her arms and nuts empty space with her head. Realizing that this is getting her nowhere she makes wiggly patterns in the air and jabs at her hand with her index finger

Margaret Sting, it's a sting; sounds like sting.

Kathy shakes her head and flaps her hand again

Fiona Wasp.

Kathy flaps frantically, encouraging them to guess more

Helen Bee?

Kathy nods wildly

Goff One minute.
Margaret Shut up you. Sounds like "bee".

Kathy nods

Helen The whole word, or is it more than one syllable? We forgot syllables!

Kathy realizes she hasn't broken the word up, smacks her forehead, stamps her foot and makes the sign for three syllables

Three syllables and the first syllable sounds like "bee".

Kathy signs "up" during Margaret's next line

Margaret Bee cee dee eee fee gee hee kee nee lee mee pee quee ree ——

Kathy nods wildly

Helen First syllable is "ree".
Fiona Second syllable.

Kathy leaps and prowls around the room clawing at the air

Goff Two minutes.
Margaret Will you shut up? You're driving us mad!
Helen Wild — sounds like wild?

Kathy shakes her head wildly

   Dog? Wolf?
Margaret Tiger?

Kathy wildly nods and flaps because they are getting close

Helen Sounds like tiger? Nothing sounds like tiger.
Goff Elijah, spider ——
Margaret I'm warning you!
Helen Not tiger?

Kathy makes the "small" sign

Margaret Small tiger.

Kathy makes the "next to" sign

Helen Next? Near? Like?

Kathy nods madly

Fiona It's like a tiger?

Kathy nods madly

Margaret Like a tiger; what's like a tiger?
Fiona A leopard?

Kathy shakes her head "no"

Helen A panther?
Fiona A lion.

Kathy nods madly

Margaret Lion; is it lion?
Kathy Yes! Yes!
Martin No talking.
Goff Half a minute.
Margaret I'll kill him — I'll kill him!
Fiona The Re — Lion? *Out of Africa*? *Born Free*?

Kathy realizes time is running out and makes the sign for the third word

   Third word.

Kathy starts to jump up and down and flap and peck at things

Margaret She's off with the birds again.
Helen Is it a type of bird?

Kathy nods madly

Fiona The relion — a type of bird?
Margaret Crow — eagle — sparrow — swan ...
Fiona Rook — crow — said that — erm — bluebird — swallow ...
Helen Parrot — chough ...

Kathy starts rubbing her chest

   Tit? It can't be tit! Is it tit?
Margaret Rely — on tits? Rely on tits?
Goff Samantha Fox did! Samantha Fox did! (*He laughs uproariously*) Ten
   seconds.
Margaret I'll kill him.
Helen The "rely — on — tit"?
Fiona It's not a tit? Another bird?
Goff Time!

Kathy It was a robin redbreast.
Margaret I've never heard of it! What kind of book's that?
Kathy Not the book, the mime.
Helen What was the book?
Kathy *The Reliant Robin Workshop Manual.*
Margaret You cheating beggers!
Martin It's not a cheat, it's a book! That's all it has to be — a book. And *The Reliant Robin Workshop Manual* is definitely a book. It's not a record or a filum or a TV show. Nor is it a play. Though I dare say some Post-Modernist eejit will turn it into one one of these days.

The women look at each other disgustedly

Margaret *The Reliant Robin Workshop Manual*! I've heard everythin' now.
Fiona Men just love to win, don't they? They can't stand to be beaten and they'll go to any length, including cheating, to win. It's worse in bloody Australia. You're lucky if they let you join in anything there and if a woman wins they sulk.
Jimmy Come on Fiona, leave it out; don't start all that stuff again.
Helen I've got one. (*She writes a note and shows it to the women*)

The women grin

Here you are Goff — your go first. (*She hands Goff the note*)

Goff reads the note and stands in the middle of the room

Margaret Three minutes starting now!

Goff mimes "a film" then "thirteen words" in the style of Marcel Marceau

Martin Film.
Jimmy Thirteen words.

Goff mimes a doctor with a stethoscope, then pulls a "strange" face, kisses the air, looks worried and terrified, makes a mushroom shape with his hands and cuddles the shape

Martin "*Dr Strangelove or How I learned to Stop Worrying and Love the Bomb*". (*He looks at his watch*) Nine seconds.
Margaret You cheating beggars!
Jimmy How was it cheating?
Kathy Well, how did you get it so quickly? I mean ... ! (*She leaves this comment in the air*)

Martin (*relishing his words*) It was — native intelligence; some of us have got it, some haven't.

Goff Talent will out; sorry, girls, that's one-nil to the lads.

Martin (*writing a note*) Here's your next one; Fiona, your go. (*He gives Fiona the note*)

Fiona How the heck do I do this?

Martin Stand on your head and feel at home. Three minutes, starting now.

Fiona mimes "a book"

Helen Book.

Margaret If it's another workshop manual I'll wring his blessed neck!

Fiona mimes "five words" then points to her wedding ring

   Mrs Beeton's Book of Household Management. (*She looks at her watch*) Eight seconds.

Martin How the hell did you get that?

Margaret It was raw intelligence; some of us have got it and some haven't.

Helen You gave us that last year.

Kathy And we got it first time then, too. OK, girls, both barrels now. Come on, Crispin, it's your go. (*She writes out a note and gives it to him during the following*)

Crispin Somebody else should go first, surely.

Kathy It'll be all right.

Martin You must have mastered the game be now.

Helen You have three minutes, starting now.

Crispin looks at the paper then makes the sign for "television"

Martin TV show.

Crispin makes the sign for "two"

Goff Two words.

Crispin then drops to a crouching position and starts hopping

Goff Donald Duck.

Jimmy The Road Runner.

Martin Chick chick chick chick chicken, lay a little egg for me.

Goff A TV programme about birds? *Emmerdale Farm*?

Crispin starts pecking and flapping

Jimmy Does it sound like something?
Margaret Two minutes.
Goff Give the bloke a break, he's new to the game.
Helen The shoe's on the other foot now.
Margaret And it's pinching.
Jimmy How many syllables in the first word?

Crispin stops hopping and thinks for a moment, then makes the sign for "four"

Martin Four syllables.

Crispin continues hopping, pecking and flapping. They all watch. He does a very good impression of a chicken laying an egg

Goff A duck having a shite?
Fiona Dad!
Goff Well, it looks like it to me! What else is it supposed to be? Try summat else, Crispin lad, we're peein' into t' wind here.
Margaret One minute.
Goff It can't be.
Martin It feels like we've been at it for years.
Jimmy (*inspired*) Clucky Lucky!
Goff Luck — something to do with luck!
Martin I haven't a bloody clue; it's as clear as Dick's Hat.
Goff Cock! Anything to do with cock? Hens.
Jimmy Cock — hens — chickens ...
Martin I give up.
Goff We can't give up.
Martin We haven't a bloody clue.
Jimmy It's on television; two words and it's to do with chickens.
Martin Wait a minute, he's bouncing round, bending down: *Red Dwarf*?
Goff What's *Red Dwarf* got to do with chickens, you daft 'tater?
Margaret Half a minute.
Goff We give up.
Jimmy We all give up.
Martin Not a bloody clue.
Crispin *Coronation Street.*
Martin (*amazed*) *Coronation Street*?
Goff *Coronation Street*; what the bloody hell has a chicken laying an egg to do with *Coronation Street*?

Crispin Well, nothing really, I suppose.

Jimmy Then what did you do it for?

Crispin Well, I thought Coronation chicken, you know — and besides, it's the only impression I can do.

Martin Jesus, Henry, Joseph and Molly! I've heard everything now. You haven't thought of getting a grant for that — performance art, you know? The concept of the chicken as victim perhaps?

Crispin (*puzzled*) No?

Margaret I think that's enough of charades. I never liked them anyway. You always give the women hard stuff to do and then moan when we beat you.

Martin I don't mind being beaten fair and square but I deeply resent being beaten by a bloody Post-Modernist chicken.

They all settle down again

(*Pouring out more drinks; to Crispin*) You're in the arts business like Kathy, then?

Crispin Well, when I left Cambridge I didn't know what I wanted to do really — for a job, that is. My degree is in fine art. My parents are very involved with Glyndebourne and I'd organized quite a few events at uni so I sort of fell into arts funding and management. I'm mainly involved with curating exhibitions now.

Martin Piles of bricks.

Crispin Ah, the pile of bricks, the favourite whipping horse of the *Sun* reader.

Martin The *Sun*, the *Sun*! I wouldn't wipe me backside on it! I read the *Guardian* and the *Independent* and the *Observer* on a Sunday. The *Sun* — I wouldn't wrap chips in it. It'd turn 'em bad.

Kathy Dad, don't get bolshie. Modern Art isn't something you just look at, you have to know all the references.

During the following, Martin is winding Crispin up, but we must be convinced of Martin's sincerity. If we know it's a wind-up it will blow the effect

Martin That's fascinating; I've never really looked at it that way before.

Crispin Well, you see a pile of bricks, but that pile is selected. The very act of selection is a statement by the artist. He is saying this brick is now all bricks that ever were or will be. This line of bricks is a wall and every wall that will be or has been.

Martin That's fascinating; I've never really looked at it that way before. But what about that sheep that was pickled in formaldehyde?

Crispin Well, you see, that illustrates so many things. At one level it is questioning reality. What is real? What is art? That sheep is dead and not dead, because it is fixed in formaldehyde. It is both being and not being, becoming and not becoming; it is death in life and life in death.

Martin That's fascinating; I've never really looked at it that way before. But what about that bloke who made a plastic mould of his own head, then filled it with his own blood and showed it as art, or that bloke who paints with elephants' turds?

Goff They're good for sprouts, are elephants' turds.

Crispin But the head filled with blood says so much about what is real and what isn't and what bodily fluids are and about the artist and his involvement with his work. In this case the artist becomes his or her work. Like the woman who has had all the plastic surgery; she sees her body as her art.

Martin That's fascinating; I've never really looked at it that way before. (*Beat*) I've been taking elocution lessons, you know.

Crispin Oh, but you mustn't try and lose that lovely Irish brogue.

Goff (*to Martin*) You've been taking elocution lessons. I didn't know that!

Martin No better man! And they're working like a dream. I used to say "Absolute and total bull shit", but now I say "That's fascinating; I've never really looked at it that way before."

There is a beat

Kathy My dad's very traditional.

Martin No, I'm not, I'm post-post-Post-Modern.

Margaret Your dad had better shut his bloody trap or he'll be post-post-post-bloody-life.

Crispin (*showing a little barb*) Which university did you learn your art appreciation at then? I suppose it was the University of Life.

Martin No, it was the Open University. I did a BA in art history. I spent fifteen years collecting "O" levels and then I decided to do a degree. I went to night classes every Wednesday night for fifteen years and did an "O" level a year. I've got Geography, History, English Lang and Lit, Chemistry, Physics, Biology, Maths; I can speak Spanish, French, German, Italian and Urdu.

Jimmy Urdu?

Martin I couldn't go on Wednesdays that year, I had to go on Thursdays and the only thing I fancied was Urdu; well, it was either that or practical wine-making and soft furnishings and I didn't fancy having the house full of rhubarb Chardonnay and tie-backs.

Margaret What's wrong with tie-backs? I like tie-backs.

Martin They're bloody daft.

Helen (*trying to brighten things up*) Uncle Goff, do one of your daft songs.

Goff Right, I'll do one of me country and western ones; it's called "I've Never Been To Bed With An Ugly Woman But I've Sure Woke Up With

a Few". No, lass, I don't fancy a song yet. Here, I'm feeling a bit peckish;
would anybody like some nibbles?
Fiona I don't know if I could eat another thing.
Margaret There's some Twiglets in the kitchen.
Goff Martin, you fill everybody's glasses while I get the nibbles.
Jimmy (*trying to make a joke*) And no more cat food; I don't want to end
up licking my own privates.

The joke doesn't go down too well

Oh, well, some you lose.

Goff goes into the kitchen

Martin pours drinks

*Goff manoeuvres the Twiglets through the hatch but does it clumsily,
dropping some in the stick insect tank. He then comes round from the kitchen,
picks the Twiglets out of the tank and puts them back in the bowl. He then goes
back in the kitchen, passes through a bowl of nuts, comes back and hands
them round*

Goff There's nuts and Twiglets; take your pick.
Crispin Wow, Twiglets! My mother used to send these to school for me; I
love them. Do you mind if I take a few?
Goff You can take 'em all for me, bonny lad, there's another box of 'em in
t' kitchen. Fill thy booits bonny lad, as my mate from Barnsley used to say.

*During the following, Goff moves round the room handing more Twiglets
round. Nobody takes them much but Crispin. Helen goes round filling
everybody's glasses*

Crispin Hey, I know a good joke. It's an Irish joke but it's not a bad one. I
mean you can take a joke can't you, Mr Duggan?
Martin It would be a poor man that couldn't take a joke against himself.
Kathy It's not one of your crude jokes about bottoms, is it, Crispin? My
mother doesn't like crude jokes. (*To the room*) He's obsessed with
bottoms. Something to do with public school, I expect.
Crispin Oh, Katherine do shut up, I'm not obsessed.
Kathy Well, you could fool me.
Margaret Shut up and let him get on with it; you'll have it dark.
Crispin Well there's an English fox, a Scots fox and an Irish fox and they
all get caught in traps by their legs.

Goff Which leg?

Crispin It's the back leg, but it doesn't really matter to the joke. Anyway the English fox says "Dammit, chaps, the gamekeeper will be here soon and if he finds us he'll shoot us and skin us and hang our skins up as a warning to the other foxes. I'm going to gnaw my leg off." And he does just that, the brave old English fox; he chews right through his own leg. Then he says "Come on," to the Jock fox and the Paddy fox, "chew through your legs, chaps." And the Jock fox says, "Och, aye, the noo, yer right," and he chews through his leg. "Come on," they say to the Paddy fox, "chew through your leg." "Begorrah, sor, and the top of the morning to you but I wouldn't be after doing that class of thing at all at all at all."

Kathy Crispin, get on with it for God's sake. You're boring.

Crispin Kathy, do shut up. So the English fox and the Jock fox scuttle away. But the English fox says to the Jock fox, "Dammit, we can't leave poor Paddy in the trap. We'll have to go back and see what we can do." And they go back and the Paddy fox is still there. "Why on earth didn't you chew through your leg?" asks the English fox. "Oh," says the Paddy fox, "Begorrah and bejasus and top of the morning to you but I've chewed through three of them already and I'm still stuck!"

Jimmy laughs a bit but not much. The rest of them make half-hearted noises, but there is a deep sense of embarrassment

Crispin I thought it was quite good.

Martin pours himself another potheen

Margaret Martin, you'd better go steady on that.

Martin (*ignoring her*) That was very good, Crispin. But it had just the teeniest hint of the Brit in it. D'you know something Crispin, this country is like all the rest of the great Empire builders: Rome, Greece, the Ottomans ...

Fiona I thought they were chairs!

Martin It's had its day. It's finished, clapped out. It's an empire hanging on by a thread to its past glory.

Helen (*looking at her watch*) It's usually after ten before this starts, isn't it?

Margaret It's that bloody jungle juice Goff brought. I'll kill that Canon O'Connor when I see him!

Crispin Yet England still has given the world so much; how many countries would have had law, education, medicine, democracy if it wasn't for the British Empire?

Martin Some of us had them already.

Margaret Martin!

Crispin What do you mean?

Martin Before the British invaded Ireland it had colleges, schools, art, a literature second to none, music and great poetry and a legal tradition that gave equal rights to women in everything, and it had divorce. It's taken us nearly a thousand years to get back where we were. (*He pauses for breath*) You see, Crispin, your problem is ...

Margaret Martin, it's Christmas Day night: WILL YOU SHUT YOUR CAKEHOLE AND LET US ALL ENJOY CHRISTMAS WITHOUT A PIGGING FIGHT!

Kathy Cakehole, again — wicked! That's marvellous. I've not heard that in years — "cakehole".

Fiona looks into Goff's bowl of Twiglets and screams

Fiona The Twiglets, the Twiglets; they're moving, they're alive!

Goff (*peering at them*) Eee, they are an' all.

Margaret What are you talking about?

Goff Look, that one's moving.

Helen Oh my God! It's a stick insect! How the hell did that get there? They were in that tank.

Goff I wondered what that tank were for. I dropped some Twiglets in as I were passin' it through th' hatch and so I gorrum out again. I wondered what them bits of grass and stuff were for.

Helen (*running over to the tank and looking in*) They've all gone every one of them. There were twelve in there. How many are left in the bowl?

Martin Two.

Margaret Oh, my God!

Helen Somebody's eaten ten stick insects.

Fiona Are they poisonous?

Helen I don't think so.

Goff It's all protein, anyroad; what are you gettin' upset about?

They all look at Crispin

Crispin Oh no. (*He stands and shakes his head*) Oh no, don't tell me I've eaten some stick insects.

Goff It looks as though you've near scoffed the bloody lot.

Crispin goes pale before our eyes and without "codding" it becomes obvious that he is going to throw up. He flees the room

Kathy (*heading for the exit*) He's going to be sick.

Kathy follows Crispin off

Margaret Should we get a doctor?
Goff Nay, let him die. It'll be one less bloody southerner.
Fiona Dad!
Goff I were only joking!

The doorbell rings and the dog barks

Martin Who the hell's that on Christmas Day night? We weren't expecting anybody.
Jimmy I'm just going to the bathroom. I think I've got a bit of stick insect stuck down the back of me throat.
Margaret I thought Crispin ate them all.
Jimmy Well, there's something stuck down there and it feels as though it's wiggling.

Jimmy exits

Helen I'll get it.

Helen exits to the front door

Fiona I do hope he doesn't get ill.
Goff He'll be all right. It's only like them widgy grubs that you all eat in Australia.
Fiona Dad, go and see how he is; he's got a very weak stomach, has Jimmy. He hates funny food; I've only just got him to eat prawns, and I have to take the eyes out of them — he says he can see them staring at him. Dad, go and see how he is.
Goff I don't know, I'm like a piggin' nursemaid.

Goff exits

Margaret (*to Martin*) You've not invited McGoldrick round, have you?
Martin He's gone to his sister's.
Margaret It'll be Goff; he invited half the bloody allotment committee round last year and they didn't go till half-five the next morning.

Helen enters with Pat and Hughie Benson

Helen These people found some keys and the woman at the presbytery said they might be yours.

Margaret Ooh, that's wonderful.

Martin Come in, come in. You're very welcome. Would you like a drink?

Pat No, thanks. We don't want to spoil your Christmas. You all look so cosy. No, we were just on our way to my daughter's with my little grandson when he dropped his Nintendo down the grid. Well, he were that upset. Hughie said, "We'll have to get it out or he'll scream the place down and ruin everybody's Christmas". Didn't you?

Throughout the following Hughie says little but the odd subdued "ay"

Hughie Ay.

Pat So with him being an engineer he got a magnet from home and we put it down the grid, didn't we, and we managed to get it out. Didn't we?

Hughie Ay.

Pat But these keys came up with it. Well, we didn't know what to do, did we?

Hughie No.

Martin Why don't you sit down?

Pat No, thank you. We've got to go now, there's a cold collation waiting for us at my daughter's. Her husband's a police inspector and they're having some friends round. Well, I said to Hughie that somebody would be missing these keys because there's a lot on them and they look important, so we knocked on the presbytery to ask, didn't we?

Hughie Ay.

Pat And what a crabby old woman came out; we go to Our Lady of Grace so she doesn't know us! Anyway after she'd stopped moaning about us knocking on her door on Christmas Day, she told us the keys were yours and gave us your address so we thought we'd drop them off on our way. My daughter only lives a couple of avenues away (*beat*) in one of the bigger houses. Her husband's an inspector.

Margaret Well, that was very nice of you, it really was. To take time off on your Christmas Day.

Pat Are you having a nice Christmas?

Margaret Well, quiet, you know, just family.

Kathy enters with a very ashen Crispin behind her

Kathy He brought them all up, we counted the heads in the bowl and there were ten so that's the lot.

Margaret (*explaining to Pat and Hughie, logically*) He ate a lot of stick insects and they didn't agree with him. Nibbles, you know. Are you sure you wouldn't like a drink?

Pat No, I'm sure; thank you very much.

Margaret What about you?

Pat He doesn't drink when he's driving, do you?
Hughie Never have.

Goff enters with another drink and a slice of cake

Oh, hallo; Happy Christmas.
Pat And to you, too. (*Beat*) Don't I know you?
Goff I don't know, but I've a feelin' I know you. Did you used to work behind the counter at Masons the ironmongers?
Pat No, I never worked there.
Goff Funny, I could swear I once saw you baggin' a pound of inch and a half round heads.
Pat No, I was always in office work. Did you used to work on the railway?
Goff Years and years ago I did.

Jimmy enters

Jimmy Hallo there. Happy Christmas.

A long long beat

Pat Oh my God! Jimmy bloody Corcoran! Well, well, well.
Jimmy Oh shit, oh shit!
Fiona Jimmy, there's no call for language like that! Who is it?
Margaret Do you two know each other?
Pat I should do: he's me husband.
Martin After the Lord Mayor's Show! This is better than the filums.
Fiona Oh my God, I don't believe this. It can't be.
Kathy Is it her? Is it his wife? Wow! Wicked!!
Helen Well, if it isn't, this is all a very elaborate and spectacularly tasteless joke. Is it her, Fiona?
Fiona I don't know; I never set eyes on her. I just knew he was married and wasn't happy.
Pat Happy? Him happy? He'll never be happy as long as his arse looks at the ground. He was always going round looking for bits of stuff. He'd shag anything that let him.
Fiona (*stung*) Oh oh!
Margaret Look, it was all thirty years ago, we mustn't get nasty; it's all water under the bridge.
Pat It might be water under the bridge but you weren't left three months pregnant by a bloke who vanished into thin air.
Fiona Three months pregnant! You never told me.

Jimmy I didn't know!

Margaret Oh, my God, on Christmas Day!

Martin Peggy, remember your blood pressure; you've not had your tablets.

Fiona I'd never have married you if I'd known!

Pat Married ... Are you the tart he ran off with? Well, you've not worn very well, have you? Married ... You can't be married, love.

Fiona We bloody well are married. (*She shows Pat her ring*) What's that, Scotch mist?

Pat Well, they must have funny laws in Australia because to get married you have to be divorced and he never divorced me.

Fiona Oh oh oh — (*she is speechless*)

Margaret (*indicating Hughie*) Well, who's this, then?

Pat My gentleman friend. (*She indicates Jimmy with a nod*) His daughter lives just round the corner from here. She doesn't know anything much about her father and looking at him now, I'm glad.

Fiona (*to Jimmy*) You bastard! You told me it had all gone through; all those letters you wrote!!

Jimmy Well, I tried, but she'd moved away, and anyway it was all over; it just didn't seem important.

Pat It's not just important, it's illegal; I could have you done. It's what is known as bigamy in the eye of the law.

Goff I knew you couldn't trust him, him and his bloody Billy Fury haircut. (*Beat*) And all that chlorine. (*Beat*) And me saw!

Pat I know who you are now; you're that daft old sod that kept coming round knockin' on the door askin' about a bloody saw.

Goff It was a Raper and Wyman.

Margaret Will you shut up about that bloody saw? This is serious.

The doorbell rings

Helen runs towards the door. A loud throbbing noise shakes the house and a pulsing yellow light floods in through the windows — the effect should be that of a space ship landing. Everyone stands, watching; Helen squeals

Martin What is it, for Christ's sake?

Helen points dumbly towards the door

> *Two "aliens" walk stiffly in. They are dressed in silver from top to toe, with domed heads and slitty eyes; the archetypal abductors. Behind them the Lights flash so that they are lit for a while like the alien at the top of the ramp in* Close Encounters of the Third Kind

Margaret *(praying)* Hail Mary full of grace the Lord is with thee — blessed art thou amongst women and blessed is the fruit of thy womb, Jesus …

(together)

Martin Does anybody know the Perfect Act of Contrition? Does anybody know it? Oh my God, I am very sorry and with all my heart … Jesus what a time to forget it …

Goff *(taking off his trousers and getting ready for the aliens)* I'll go to the foot of our stairs. Well, don't say Goff Sedgewick wasn't ready to do his bit for the master race when the time came. Up lads and at 'em.

Pat *(to Goff)* You filthy old man!!

Kathy Wow — wicked.

Hughie *(to the "aliens")* Get back in the car.

Pat We told you to wait there.

The aliens take off their heads to reveal two kids aged about twelve, a boy and a girl

Boy We was dead bored.

Girl And I wanted a wee.

Goff Bloody hellfire.

Pat Hughie, we're going; this house is full of child molesters and adulterers.

Margaret Wasn't it a flying saucer?

Hughie Gritter; Council gritter. They don't use spaceships yet for gritting.

Pat Come on, kids. These people are mental.

Pat, Hughie and the kids exit

Kathy Goff, why precisely did you take your trousers off?

Martin He thought he was about to have sex with an alien.

Goff It's all on account of Meals on Wheels and sanitaryware accountants.

Margaret Put your trousers on!

Kathy Do you often have sex with aliens?

Goff No, it would have been my first time.

Helen He sees himself as the possible father of a race of archangels.

Kathy *(now totally confused but still wanting to seem as though she understands)* Wow — wicked — archangels yeah.

Fiona *(crying)* I'm not really married and our children are bastards.

Crispin Does anybody mind if I help myself to a drink?

Crispin pours himself a large glass of what he thinks is lemonade but which is in fact potheen. He drinks it and drops to the floor, spark out

The dog and the cat can be heard chasing each other round the room. The tree falls over. Mayhem is loosed. Water from Martin's tap comes pouring through the ceiling

CURTAIN

FURNITURE AND PROPERTY LIST

Only the furniture and properties mentioned in the text are listed here. Further items may be added at the director's discretion

ACT I
SCENE 1

On stage: FRONT ROOM
Settee
Armchair
Television
Drinks cabinet with glasses, bottles of Black Bush, Bushmills, sherry,
  cans of beer *et cetera*
Aquarium with stick insects
Box of stick insect food
Television remote control unit
Telephone
Christmas decorations, tree lights, baubles *et cetera*
Piece of Bacofoil
Can of Boddington's for **Goff**
Glass for **Goff**

KITCHEN
Tea things (several sets)
Piece of celery for **Goff** (ACT I SCENE 2)
Glass of water for **Martin** (ACT II SCENE 1)
Bottle of champagne, bucket of ice (ACT II SCENE 1)
Bowls of "cat food" nibbles for **Goff** (ACT II SCENE 2)
Bowl of Twiglets for **Goff** (ACT II SCENE 3)
Bowl of nuts for **Goff** (ACT II SCENE 3)
Drink and slice of cake for **Goff** (ACT II SCENE 3)

Off stage: Four full Tesco bags (**Margaret**)
More Tesco bags (**Margaret**, **Goff** and **Helen**)
Enormous Christmas tree (**Martin**)

Personal: **Helen**: lighter

SCENE 2

Strike: Tea things

Off stage: Bag of greens (**Goff**)

SCENE 3

Strike: Tea things

Set: Candles (lit)

Off stage: Drinks (**Martin, Helen, Margaret, Goff, Fiona**)

ACT II
SCENE 1

Strike: Christmas tree with needles

Set: Needle-less Christmas tree with lights and baubles
                   Bowl of cereal, spoon for **Helen**
                   Tea tray

Off stage: Bag of greens, including cucumber, two small turnips, two sprouts
                      (**Goff**)
                   Huge full lemonade bottle (**Goff**)
                   Cat baskets (**Kathy**)

SCENE 2

Strike: Cereal bowl, spoon, bag of greens, tea tray

Set: Presents:
                   Tie for Crispin (**Helen**)
                   Sweater for Fiona (**Helen**)
                   Sweater for Jimmy (**Kathy**)
                   Black lace slip and matching bra and pants for Margaret (**Helen**)
                   Reader's Digest Do-it-Yourself Manual for Martin (**Helen**)
                   Gardener's diary, Uncle Joe's Mint Balls, "The World's Worst Jokes"
                      for Goff (**Kathy**)
                   Duvet jacket for Helen (**Kathy**)
                   Brooch, chain and sweater for Kathy (**Kathy**)
                   Socks and two ties for Crispin (**Kathy**)

Tie for Crispin (**Helen**)
Boxer shorts for Martin (**Helen**)
Long dress for Margaret (**Kathy**)
Bow tie for Crispin (**Helen**)
Tie for Crispin (**Goff**)
Lamp for Helen (**Kathy**)
Brooch for Kathy (**Helen**)
Bath oil and CD for Kathy (**Helen**)
Saw for Goff (**Helen**)
NB The name in brackets is of the person taking the present from beneath the tree and handing it on

SCENE 3

Strike: Presents

Set: Pen, pieces of paper

LIGHTING PLOT

Practical fittings required: Christmas tree lights, TV flicker effect
One interior. The same throughout

ACT I, Scene 1

To open: General interior lighting; evening effect. TV flicker

Cue 1	**Martin** switches on the tree lights *Tree lights burn brightly*	(Page 14)
Cue 2	**All**: "Merry Christmas." *All lights flicker, slowly at first, then faster*	(Page 14)
Cue 3	Dull bang *Snap off all lights and TV*	(Page 14)
Cue 4	**Helen** lights a lighter *Covering glow on lighter*	(Page 15)
Cue 5	**All**: "Will you bugger off?" Lighter goes out *Black-out*	(Page 15)

ACT I, Scene 2

To open: General interior lighting; morning effect

Cue 6	**Jimmy**: "Saw? Saw?" *Black-out*	(Page 22)

ACT I, Scene 3

To open: General interior lighting; evening effect. Christmas tree lights on. TV flicker

Cue 7	**Helen** turns the TV off *Cut TV flicker*	(Page 25)
Cue 8	Dull explosion *Black-out*	(Page 33)

ACT II, Scene 1

To open: General interior lighting; morning effect. Christmas tree lights on. TV
  flicker

Cue 9   **Fiona** sings, the others look puzzled   (Page 46)
               Black-out

ACT II, Scene 2

To open: General interior lighting; morning effect. Christmas tree lights on

Cue 10   **Margaret**: "Buggering bloody sod Christmas!"   (Page 52)
               Black-out

ACT II, Scene 3

To open: General interior lighting; late afternoon/ early evening effect. Christmas
  tree lights on

Cue 11   Loud throbbing noise   (Page 68)
               Pulsing yellow light though windows

Cue 12   Aliens walk in   (Page 68)
               Lights through window flash

Cue 13   Christmas tree falls over   (Page 70)
               Cut Christmas tree lights

EFFECTS PLOT

ACT I

Cue 14	**Helen**: " ... while you sort it out." *"Deck the Halls" begins*	(Page 12)
Cue 15	The decoration of the room is completed *"Deck the Halls" stops*	(Page 12)
Cue 16	**Martin**: " ... take a dog like that seriously?" *Dog comes up to house and runs around inside it*	(Page 13)
Cue 17	Lights flicker faster and faster *Dull bang*	(Page 14)
Cue 18	**Margaret**: " ... happen all bloody day." *Children sing "Away in a Manger"*	(Page 15)
Cue 19	**All**: "Will you bugger off!" *Children stop singing*	(Page 15)
Cue 20	**Helen**: "Hallo ——" *Dog barks*	(Page 18)
Cue 21	**Margaret**: "I'll make some tea." *Demented dog yapping*	(Page 19)
Cue 22	**Margaret**: "Goff — give us a break." *Doorbell*	(Page 24)
Cue 23	**Margaret**: " ... go and get the door." *Doorbell*	(Page 25)
Cue 24	**Fiona** jumps up and screams hysterically *Dog barks*	(Page 29)
Cue 25	**Martin** pulls the tree down *Carol singers sing "Jingle Bells".* *Dull explosion with smoke from the tree*	(Page 33)

ACT II

Cue 26	As the Curtain rises *Carols from TV*	(Page 36)
Cue 27	**Goff**: " ... the blood's all settled in your head." *Doorbell*	(Page 38)
Cue 28	**All**: "Happy Christmas." *Doorbell; mad dog sounds*	(Page 40)

Cue 29	**Margaret** points towards the kitchen *Dog barks*	(Page 42)
Cue 30	**Margaret**: "Good girl." *Barking, meowing, hissing, yelping from dog and cats*	(Page 43)
Cue 31	**Margaret**: " —— go and fix it." *Yapping and hissing, continuing; fade out p.44*	(Page 43)
Cue 32	**Goff**: "I were only joking." *Doorbell; dog barks*	(Page 65)
Cue 33	**Margaret**: "This is serious." *Doorbell; then loud throbbing noise*	(Page 68)
Cue 34	**Crispin** falls to the floor *Dog and cat noises. Water pours through the ceiling*	(Page 69)